*Real People, Rea*

# Sky Windows

MAGICAL, MYSTICAL, MARVELOUS MOMENTS

Kathleene Keidel

by **Kathleene Keidel** *with Contributing Authors*

## DEDICATION

For Marge, my favorite M.A.D. Hatter

***To all those who find meaning when looking through their own sky windows.***

---

"Be watchful
The grace of God appears suddenly
It comes without warning
To an open heart."
—Rumi

*ISBN: 978-1-7373751-0-4 (softcover)*
*ISBN: 978-1-7373751-1-1 (ebook)*

*Library of Congress Control Number: 2021911692*

*Printed in the United States of America*

*Cover and interior design by Joanna Price, Mayfly Design*

*Front cover and title page image by Noppanun K, Shutterstock*

## TABLE OF CONTENTS

# INTRODUCTION

Why? How? What If? Does it Matter? Now what?

These are some of the questions you may ask yourself if you have had a spiritual experience. These experiences may have felt like a magical, mystical, or marvelous moment in time. Some individuals may have experienced one such moment, while others may have experienced many such moments throughout their lifetime.

In contemplating many of my own experiences, I believe that some experiences are a connection to something larger than ourselves. This may be defined as connecting to the Divine Source, or God, or Grace, or something palpable yet undefinable. Some experiences may be life-altering. Ultimately, I believe spiritual experiences are a connection to our greatest purpose in life: Love.

Other people may have had experiences that were extraordinary, but not necessarily connected to a feeling of Divine love. Some of these experiences may have been merely brief moments or what others may pass off as trivial. Yet, no matter how trivial they may seem, I consider them "nudges." If one pays close attention to these nudges, perhaps a deeper meaning can be attributed to the experience. Consider a magical, mystical, or marvelous experience an awakening to the marvel of the mysteries in life.

While at one time, science may have disregarded such experiences as a function or dysfunction of the brain, these experiences are now acceptable discussions in both science and spirituality circles as the truth of someone's

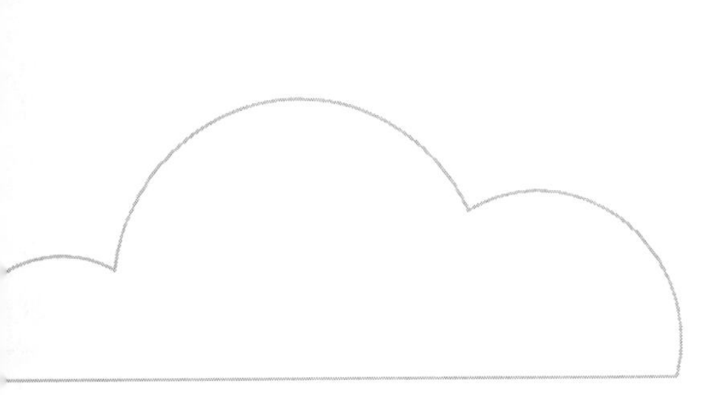

personal experience. Throughout history, millions of people across the planet have reported experiencing unexplained phenomena.

The extraordinary moments take many forms: Clairvoyance, claircognizant, clairaudience, clairalience, precognition, premonition, astral projection, lucid dreaming, animal or nature spirit, visual or auditory hallucination, near-death experience, after-death experience, telepathy, angel guardian, spirit visitation, automatic writing or automatic drawing, dreams, serendipity or synchronicity, or Divine intervention.

I first began experiencing life in extraordinary moments when I was twelve years old. I had been an extremely empathetic child, and as I got older, I realized that being a psychic empath did not need to be scary. For years I refrained from sharing my experiences, worried about how I would be perceived or how my experiences would be received by others.

When the COVID-19 pandemic struck in 2019, and stay-at-home orders went into effect in 2020, I began to think about my experiences as spiritual gifts. This project had tugged at my heartstrings for years and so I began recording all the experiences I could remember into one tidy collection. After recording these experiences, I solicited stories from others. That others were eager to share their experiences with me gave their stories a home. If in my circle alone I received these responses, I realized there must be many folks in the world who haven't shared their experiences yet who might find comfort

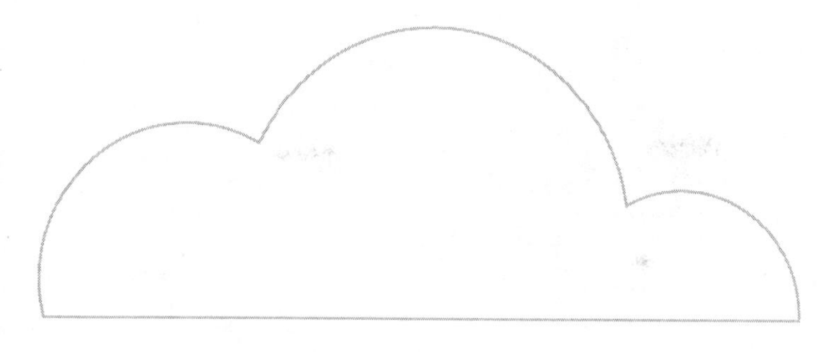

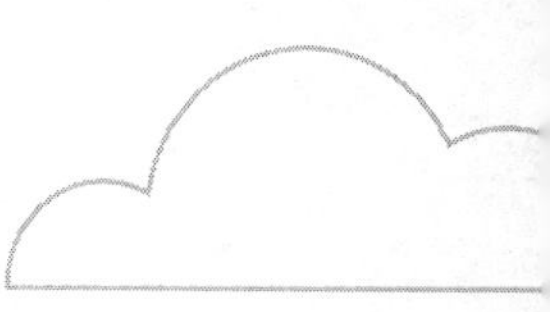

and camaraderie in the experiences of others. At that point, the concept of writing this book for the mass market was formed.

At the end of the book I have included journaling pages. The experience of another may jog a memory for the reader, so the provided spaces are for personal reflections.

A special thank you goes out to the authors who trusted me with their stories for inclusion in this book. Reading each story affirmed the purpose of this book. I value each of you and recognize how powerful your experience is to you. Thank you also to each reader. You are immersing yourself in these pages for a reason.

Above all, I hope you can view magical, mystical, and marvelous moments as I do: They are a gift. They are coming from a place of wisdom and knowledge from deep within our souls. Please consider the experiences more meaningful than coincidental and keep your sky window open!

With gratitude,
***Kathleene Keidel***

*Chapter One*

# Synchronicity & Serendipity

# Two Men on a Mountain

***(From interviews with Mike Gallagher and David Bott)***

Who would have guessed a special friendship would be forged at the bottom of an eighty-foot embankment in the mountains of Colorado?

For Mike Gallagher, the day began with a plan to take a motorcycle ride up Cottonwood Pass. He was mourning the loss of his beloved dog, Gertie, who had tragically perished after ingesting toxins. A motorcycle ride at dusk on a cool June night would help clear his head, but in his haste, he left for his ride without his usual leather riding gear. He simply donned jeans, a helmet, and a lightweight jacket. As he rode up the pass, preoccupied with the trauma of his loss, he was oblivious to the scenery or the steep curves. Before he knew it, he was careening off the edge of the mountain road, his doomed motorcycle somersaulting into empty space.

*The next day, Dave Bott was cycling on another sort of bike—a racing bike—pedaling fast up the same pass. He was on his own time trial, with specific goals. As his wheels spun around a curve, he caught a glimpse of skid marks—not an unusual sight for mountain roads. Dave picked up his pace, but as he did so, he heard a voice in his head, "Go back." Dave was not to be deterred from pursuing his goal, so he ignored the voice and pedaled harder. "Go back!" the voice commanded louder as he continued up the pass.*

*A mile up the road, Dave began to argue with the voice in his head. "I am not going back," he said.*

*"Go back, NOW!" the voice insisted. Dave relented, not knowing why but accepting that he must heed the voice.*

As Mike spun out of control, his body shot like a rocket toward a tree. Spontaneously, he flung his arm up in front of his face to shield the impact. The branches grabbed at his left arm, ripping it from its socket. As he fell to the ground, the tree landed on top of him, his arm twisted behind his back. Then, his motorcycle landed on top of the tree, the weight of it pressing against his body, severing his left leg. To make matters worse, even more tree branches landed on top of the motorcycle. Mike was sandwiched between the ground, tree, motorcycle, and branches. Gasoline began leaking onto his body, searing his skin with first-degree burns. Yet miraculously, the heat of the gasoline saved him from hypothermia and, along with all the weight pressing into him, cauterized the open wounds that were grievous enough to cause him to bleed out. As Mike lay pinned to the ground, he knew his situation was dire. He could hear the passing motorists on the road above and tried to call out for help but in vain. Three of Mike's four limbs were rendered useless. With his one good arm, he reached for the 1800s Sacred Heart of Jesus metal plate on his motorcycle. It had belonged to a grandfather he had never met, who had kept the plate in a sea chest in his native Ireland.

Mike explained to me, "To the world, that metal plate is just a badge. But to me, it has always been a spiritual connection to my belief in God." As dusk turned to darkness, he lay alone on the cold ground. He placed his hand on top of the plate, his touchstone. Immediately he felt warmth, comfort, and love. "Then," he reflected, "I thought of my life. I had tried to live a good life. I felt peace in that and was ready to be judged. It was Go-Time for me, so I recited my own version of the Bible's *Twenty-third Psalm*."

When he finished the Psalm, he clearly heard in his mind, "We are going to fight this together." He believed the message came from a close friend who had died in a car accident after being struck by a drunk driver. Mike said once he heard the message, he had no doubt he would be rescued. Over the next twenty-four hours, those heroic "angels" began arriving, one by one, all to aid in his rescue. There was synchronicity in the events that followed his crash.

*When Dave reached the skid marks, he lay his bike on the ground and looked over the edge of the curve. He could not see anything. He slid down the embankment and began exploring. Then, he saw movement, something black. After realizing it was a helmet, he caught sight of the downed tree and mangled motorcycle. Dave shimmied quickly to the person he found struggling to move under the wreckage, and his outdoor survival and emergency training kicked into high gear. When he reached Mike, he was met with one desperate plea, "Please, get this motorcycle off of me!"*

*But Dave knew not to do so. "I can't do that, Buddy. Your injuries are too severe." While Dave assessed Mike's injuries, he noticed that Mike had used a key to try to saw the tree from his leg. Mike's vitals were weak; the situation was dire and urgent, but in that moment, a strong feeling told Dave to stay with Mike for those first few minutes. He tried to offer comfort and words of encouragement. But then, another feeling soon overwhelmed him, and he knew he had to hurry back to the top of the hill to seek help. As soon as he reached the top, he flagged down a car with an elderly couple. At 10,700 feet in elevation, there was no cell phone service, so Dave directed the couple to drive to cell phone service range ten miles down the pass and to "call for all emergency resources." The next vehicle Dave flagged down was a pickup truck loaded with kayaks and a family for four. The driver told Dave he had served in the military as a trauma surgeon and was currently working in a local Colorado hospital. The doctor jumped into action with Dave and took control over all directives for the remainder of the rescue.*

Meanwhile, two other local doctors, Dr. Ruiter and Dr. Johnson, who both worked for Chaffee County Search and Rescue, were five minutes away up the pass on a training mission at an elevation of 12,000 feet. When they received the call via satellite phones, they jumped into action. Dr. Ruiter was Director of Communications for Chaffee County Search and Rescue and was able to reach out to all emergency vehicles.

Within a short amount of time, emergency vehicles arrived on the scene. The Search and Rescue firetruck had a new hydraulic line that was instrumental in safely cutting the tree, far more effective than the Jaws for Life in this precarious situation. The helicopter deployed was a brand new one licensed for difficult rescues. The pilot, Travis Durbin, had the credentials to maneuver the helicopter in dangerous and challenging mountainous regions.

Mike said, "All the agencies cooperated in the rescue. There was a sense of spirituality present that engulfed the rescue mission. That can't be denied. It was as if a spiritual beacon of light went out that day, and all the best people joined together with the equipment necessary for the conditions. It was almost as if they were hand-picked that day. I don't know why this happened. But I don't question it. I believe there is a path for us all. Even with all the unrest in the world, I believe there is a path for us to stay on; to live our best lives. The heroes in this story were doing just that."

Once in the helicopter, Mike's lung had to be inflated; he was paddled twice. He spent forty-one days in an induced coma with multiple internal and external traumatic injuries. But with the excellent medical care he received, he survived. Mike noted, "Against the odds, I emerged from rehab at the end of six months, able to walk and live independently." Today, with one good limb, you still might find him back on his motorcycle, dirt biking, or skiing. It is only because a stranger heeded the words, "Go back," that Mike is alive today. And Dave? Well, you just might find him racing up the pass, on his way to his best time trial yet.

"There are two ways to live your life. If nothing is a miracle and if everything is a miracle."

—ALBERT EINSTEIN

# My World Record

**JEFF KEIDEL**

*This true story is one that I tell my high school biology students on the first day of school to introduce myself... and to have some fun.*

I hold a world record. No kidding. It is a record I have held since 1969. Few world records last fifty-one years. I imagine that my world record will last at least another fifty-one years, and probably forever. What is amazing is that I did not know I held this world record until an unlikely revelation at the Morgan Library on the campus of Colorado State University in 1978.

But first, a little about my childhood. From my birth in 1958 until my late teens, I spent every summer, nearly all summer, on my grandmother's farm on Nantucket Island, Massachusetts. It wasn't a real farm, but it used to be. In fact, the farmhouse was built before the Revolutionary War. The area around the farmhouse, called Polpis, was still quite rural with lots of open space, some fields, tangled thickets, "Hidden Forests," swamps, and cranberry bogs. It was the perfect playground for a young boy. Our family's farm mantra was, "Work in the morning, and play in the afternoon." So, most days after lunch, my cousins and I would go "mess around" in the Polpis area. That typically meant riding our bikes or going on foot to explore and look for adventure. We would often be gone all afternoon and return home for dinner. One of our favorite things to do was to catch critters: frogs, crabs, birds, turtles, and snakes.

The rarer, meaner, and bigger the creature, the higher our social rank would be for the day. Often, we would bring the critters back and put them in a box in the barn after first terrorizing my sisters with a surprise under their bed covers. On my fifteenth birthday, my grandmother gave me the first edition of *Field Guide to Reptiles and Amphibians* by Dr. Roger Conant. I used it to help identify the critters we caught. I still have that book on my bookshelf today.

Fast forward. After high school, I attended Colorado State University in Fort Collins, Colorado. I was in the School of Forestry and Natural Resources with some vague idea of becoming a forest ranger. One night I went to the library to study. Well, I went under the auspices of studying. But really, I went there to check out a girl from my botany class that I heard studied there, and I hoped I would find some excuse to accidentally bump into her to "study-buddy" for an upcoming test.

Morgan Library, like many others at major universities, is huge. There were rows and rows of books and other resources. So, it took me quite a while to search for a study nook that might hold the object of my interest. I thought that I saw her from a distance but was not sure if that was her. So, I worked my way down one of the aisles, found a gap in the books, and peeked around. I still wasn't quite sure, so I moved in closer to another gap in a bookshelf. Yep. It was she. So, I took a breath to move in.

But before I did, I happened to glance at the book that my right hand was brushing against. Instantly, I completely lost all interest in the girl and become focused on the book. The title was *This Broken Archipelago* by James Lazell Jr. It was published in 1969. I was in the natural history section of the library, and for biologists, islands and archipelagos are of particular interest in the evolution of species. After all, it was the Galapagos Islands that set the stage for Darwin's masterpiece.

The subtitle of the book was "Cape Cod and the Islands, Amphibians and Reptiles." The cover showed various photos of frogs, turtles, snakes, and lizards set against a graphic map of the eastern seaboard of Massachusetts. The book was certainly not a best seller and had a limited reading audience of bio geeks, but to me, it was an amazing discovery.

As I flipped through the book, skimming the academic discussion of the possible causes of the archipelago's reptile and amphibian populations, on page 206, I found a photo of an eastern milk snake. That was one of the prettier and larger species of snakes that I caught as a kid in Polpis. On the next page was this paragraph:

*"In the first edition of the Field Guide, Dr. Conant listed only 47 ¼ inches (as the record length). Jeff Keidel caught a 52-inch male at Polpis and gave it to me on 16 July 1969. It lived awhile in captivity but probably did not grow. When it died, I put it in the Museum of Comparative Zoology at Harvard. It is fitting that a Nantucket specimen should hold the record..."*

I was in shock at seeing my name. In 1969, I was eleven years old. After a deep excavation into my memory, I remembered that day. My cousins and I were at the farm and some "college boys" stopped by (James Lazell Jr. graduated from Harvard). They explained that they were doing some research on animals on the islands. The details of that conversation were way over my eleven-year-old head, but when they asked if we could take them out and show them where to hunt for critters, I was excited! We spent the next several hours tromping around the swamps and fields, and truthfully, I can't remember if we caught anything. But I remember, when we came back at the end of the day, giving one of the guys a great big milk snake that I had caught the day before.

A quick check of my old *Field Guide to Reptiles and Amphibians* confirms that the record length for an eastern milk snake was, in fact, forty-seven and a quarter inches. The most recent edition (third) published in 1998 now lists the record at fifty-two inches. That is my fifty-two-inch milk snake! Googling eastern milk snake today, any number of websites will also show that the record length is fifty-two inches. The record has stood for fifty-one years.

If only that girl in the library could see me now.

I have been studying biology ever since I was eleven years old. No wonder I am a biology teacher today!

"Life is not measured in breaths we take, but in the moments that take our breath away."

—MAYA ANGELOU

# A Medical Revelation

I had been taking the antibiotic Levaquin for chronic bronchitis on and off for a couple of months. The bronchitis cleared up, and as I began to resume my exercise, which included running several miles each day, I noticed pain in the heels of both my feet. Upon closer examination, I saw that not only were my Achilles tendons sore, but they were also extremely swollen. I had to stop exercising and began treating the inflammation with ice and heat every evening. I scheduled an appointment with a specialist, and my friend, Julie, offered to drive me to my appointment.

On the day of the appointment, we had some extra time to kill and decided to stop at a bookstore to browse. After a few minutes, Julie approached me with a book on medications and side effects—of all things to find in a small bookstore! I placed it on a nearby table and began perusing medications and decided to look up Levaquin. I was amazed to read that the medication was known to cause tendonitis and even rupture of the Achilles tendon! I equipped myself with this information, jotting down a few notes, and proceeded to my appointment.

I mentioned my newly procured information to the specialist and was quite surprised that he simply said, "Well, that is controversial. There is no research to actually document that." However, I stopped the medication and have never taken it since then, and both of my Achilles tendons healed. Since that time, it has now been well-documented that the medication can indeed cause ruptures. In fact, several years later, it was taken off the market.

"A pure heart open to the light will be filled with the very essence of truth."

—RUMI

# Who But?

## AUDREY SMITH

"A rose by any other name would smell as sweet," said William Shakespeare. I like the name Divine Providence above all the serendipities, synchronicities, and coincidences of life that explain just a few interventions on my behalf: behind the scenes and on full stage.

When I was four years old, I had a severe head injury. Mother gave into my pleadings to cross Barstow Avenue in Eau Claire, Wisconsin, to visit the candy store. A physician's vehicle hit me, fracturing my skull. After the quick attention from the doctor and three days in a coma, I healed. It was fortunate that a doctor was the cause of the accident since he was the reason I received the immediate medical attention needed.

Who woke up our daughter, Amiejoy, asleep at the wheel that early morning driving home after a late night spent creating a photo collage for her grandmother? Who guided her into a mercifully wide, grassy median and safely back onto Interstate 94?

How did my nine-year-old brother, Ron, and I, at thirteen years, escape serious injury or destruction on our frequent careenings in the tongue of our open farm wagon, steering in and out of the curves of Mineral Springs Hill in Owatonna, Minnesota?

What kept our Smith family van from slipping over the edge of Bolivia's gravely, single-lane mountain roads to join the other unfortunate vehicles rusting out in the ravine far below?

Who whittled, challenged, affirmed, and loved me over these eighty-eight years with my dear husband, Doug, our five thriving children—Doug Loren, Kirsten Ann, Alysan Mae, Leith Daniel, and Amiejoy Caroline, along with unique friends from other cultures and many walks of life?

I am grateful this 2020 Thanksgiving during the COVID-19 pandemic for the creative ways to stay close at a distance. Our grandson, Joash, created a video of thanksgiving for our full family—far and near. Pumpkin and apple pies waited on our doorsteps, reminding us we are loved and not forgotten.

Now at Advent, I am grateful to remember my Messiah, who stepped over space to offer salvation and purpose to my life.

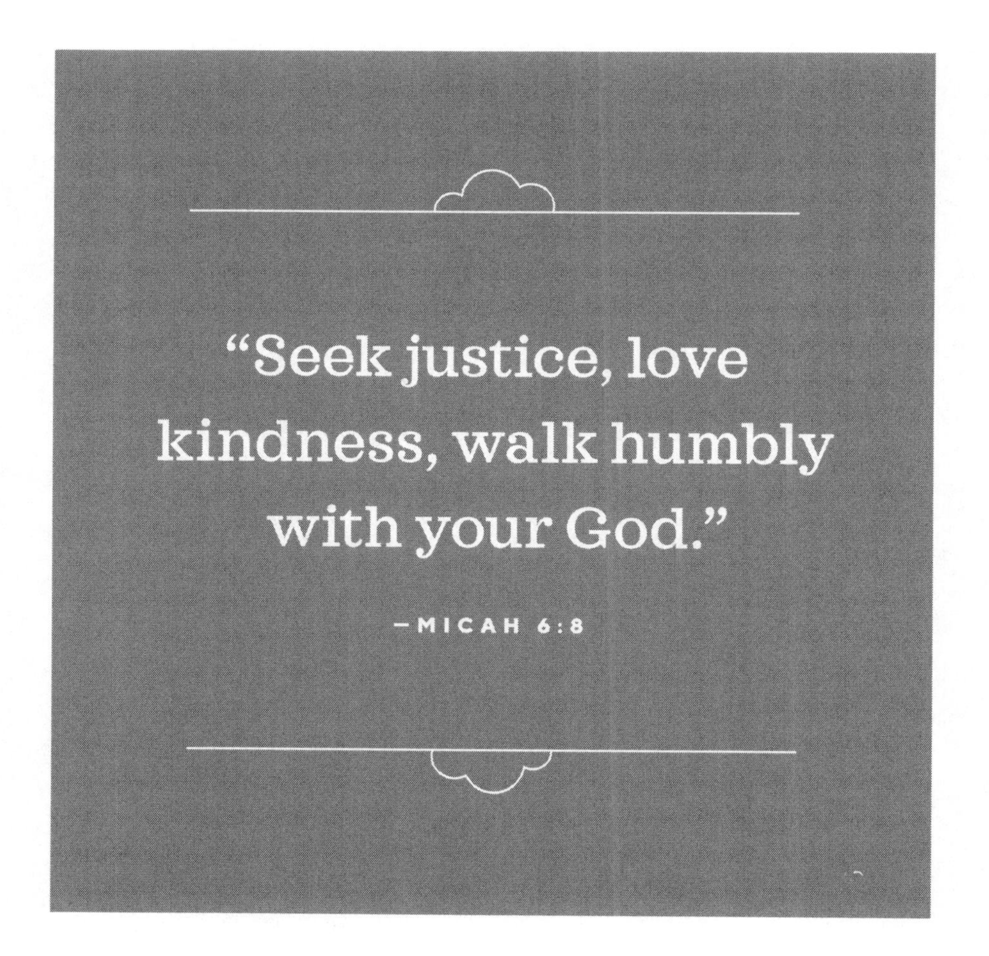

"Seek justice, love kindness, walk humbly with your God."
—MICAH 6:8

# Not Wasted on the Way

A large group of us met for a family reunion in the Boundary Waters Canoe Area. Everything about that trip was magical, as is often the case when exploring new places. We all crowded into a cabin the night before we were to begin our canoe trip onto the lakes. We slept on the hard, wooden floor on camping pads and sprawled anywhere that twelve people could comfortably sprawl in sleeping bags. The trick was getting up in the middle of the night and tiptoeing over people to get to the outhouse.

When I could wait no longer, I did just that. As quietly as possible, I made my way to the door and outside to follow the lighted pathway to the outhouse. I stopped for a moment and listened to the loons softly calling on the lake. With the light of the moon reflecting on the waters, I felt a sense of peace. Then as I made my way along the pathway through the trees, I heard music. It was coming from the outhouse. I entered the small space to find an old radio on the floor, with the song, "Wasted on the Way," by Crosby, Stills, and Nash, floating around me. The lyrics, "And there's so much time to make up everywhere you turn, time we have wasted on the way, so much water moving underneath the bridge, let the water come and carry us away."

I contemplated these words. Tomorrow the waters would be carrying us away. My husband and I needed this time, as relationships can ebb and flow, and I had secretly hoped this trip might help rekindle some sense of unity and adventure in us again. The lyrics of the song spoke to me. How easy it is for us all to waste time on trivial things. There was so much time to make up. The water would be carrying us away in the morning. The song was a metaphor for me. It was a farewell to the old, a welcoming of new possibilities. I could hear the words in my mind for the entire trip and will always appreciate the gift of that moment—the night in the outhouse, the loons chiming in agreement—as I walked back to the cabin, renewed, hopeful.

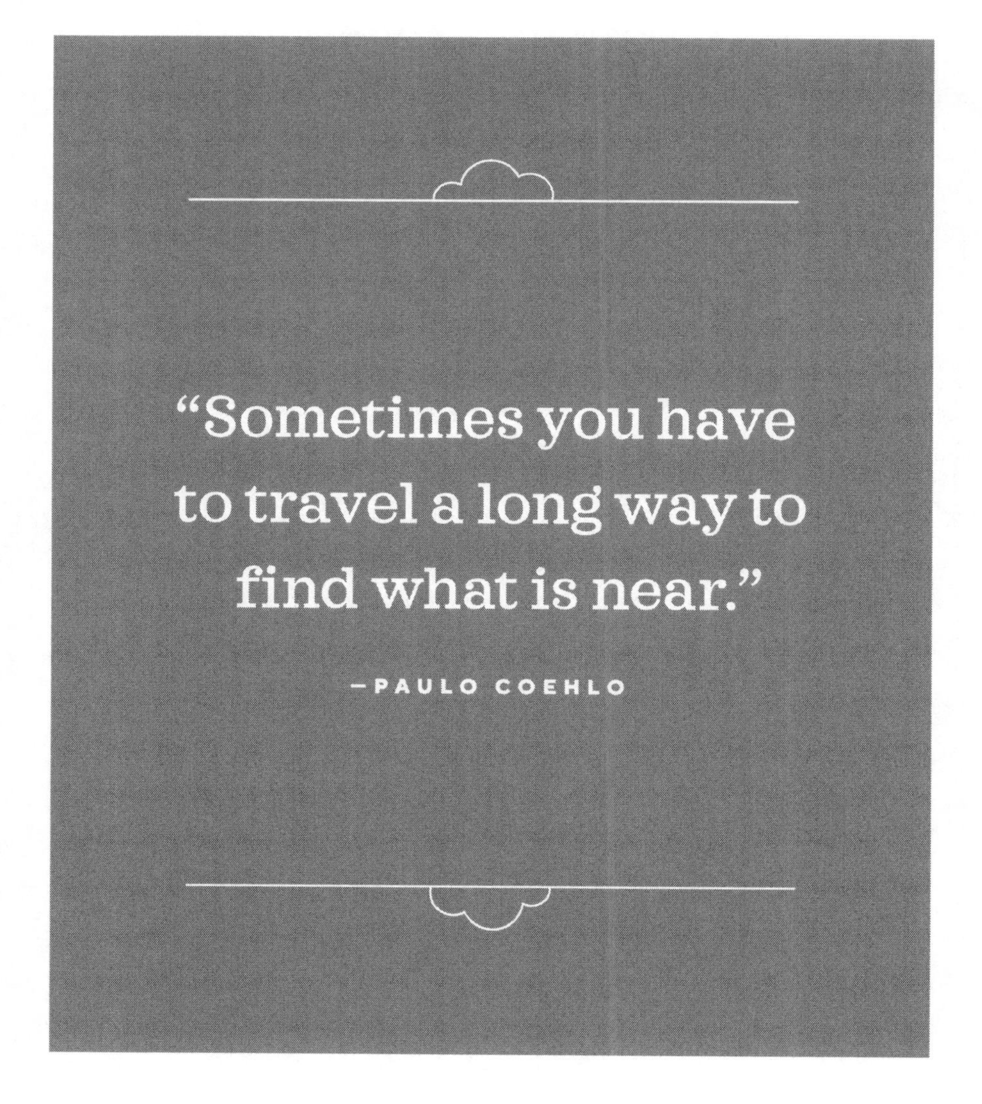

"Sometimes you have to travel a long way to find what is near."
—PAULO COEHLO

# Under the Boughs of the Trees

It was one of my first trips to visit my daughter and her husband in Alaska, shortly after they had moved there. The state was magnificent, and I could see why it was called The Last Frontier, the 49$^{th}$ state of the Union, with its vast expanse of remote and undisturbed landscape. Known also as The Land of the Midnight Sun, I was in awe, experiencing Alaska at midnight in the summer, with a light that was dim on the horizon through sunrise.

With both my daughter and son-in-law at work one day, I enjoyed a walk along a concrete path outside the wooded areas within the city of Anchorage. I had bear spray and bells on my backpack and was advised what to do should I encounter a bear or moose. There were other hikers that day, so I was not particularly concerned, but I stayed aware and avoided the temptation to veer off into the forested trails adjacent to my path.

Ahead of me was a beautiful bough of trees. It was like a tunnel of trees, I mused. Just as I reached the overhanging boughs, music emanated from my cell phone, when minutes earlier, it had been silent in my pocket. I listened to the chorus of the lovely song playing. It was not familiar to me, but the words I caught astounded me. They spoke of following a path under the boughs of trees, just as I was doing in that moment. Ultimately, it was a song of love. They were words I needed to hear.

“The light of consciousness is all that is necessary; you are the light.”

—ECKART TOLLE

# Mother

**NANCY WALTERS**

It was my habit when I lived in rural Colorado to take early morning walks, particularly down a dirt road that faced the massive range of the Collegiate Peaks. On one of those walks, I ruminated about my mother and our ragged relationship. In my early childhood, she often referred to me as "the brat" and even hired a neighbor, a young teenage girl, six or more years older than me, to be a playmate. As I grew older and started to excel in school, Mom began bragging about me to her friends, often in my presence. She helped me out when I failed at making a prom dress without a pattern by convincing my dad to pay for a store-bought gown. We continued uncomfortably close for the next fifty-seven years, through my marriage, her moving with Dad to Florida, and the birth of her grandchildren in Colorado.

On that early morning walk in August of 2010, I contemplated this inner turmoil. Why did we have so much difficulty connecting lovingly? Her attitude towards me, my lack of genuine caring, and my anger about this were old, unresolved grievances. I turned around and walked home.

Two months later, on a sunny October morning, I joined my writing friends in the courtyard of **Mother's**—a small, local restaurant in the downstairs of an old, historic hotel. My cell phone rang; I answered and heard my father telling me the news. My **mother** had died from a stroke during the night.

"A journey of
a thousand miles,
Begins with a
single step."

—LAO TZU

# A Surprise Gift

TYLER KEIDEL

Recently I ordered my two-year-old nephew a baseball cap. I had unlimited choices from the company my sister liked, but I decided on one that I thought he and his mother would like. After my tracking slip showed that it had been delivered, I called my sister and asked if they had received a package from me yet. She said they had not. So began the search for the "missing package."

After about a week, my sister called and asked, "Did you send a hat?" And when I confirmed yes, that was the surprise package, she said, "Oh! I'm so sorry! I did receive that package! I was so confused because I had ordered that very same hat from the same company but canceled the order when I realized the hat was on back order. So, when I received it, I thought it was sent by mistake since that was the order I had canceled! Thank you—we love it!"

I was happy she finally received the gift, but surprised that with the number of style options available, the hat I ordered was the very same hat she had intended to order!

“Even the silence has
a story to tell you.
Listen. Listen. Listen.”

—JACQUELINE WOODSON

# Answered Prayers

**AMBER WALKER**

In my mid-thirties, I flew from Alaska to Denver, Colorado, to be with a close friend as she was undergoing surgery for ovarian cancer. She needed several surgeries, and I stayed at the hospital with her around the clock, except when I would walk to nearby restaurants to grab food for her visitors and family members. She was in a lot of pain and experienced several post-operative complications; it was an emotional time for everyone.

I found myself lying awake one night in her hospital room, distracted by thoughts about a past relationship that had ended poorly nearly six years prior. I was puzzled as to why the relationship with this man (let's call him "Andrew") was on my mind. At the time, I was happily in love and had not thought about Andrew very often. I was more concerned with what was going on with my hospitalized friend, so it bothered me that he was suddenly on my mind.

I hadn't seen Andrew since we'd ended the relationship. We had been close friends since we were teenagers, and part of the pain of the breakup was mourning the loss of our deep friendship. I began to think about the things that I had wished I could have said to him; I realized I'd never had closure. He had cut off all communications with me the day of the breakup when he'd chosen to pursue someone else, and it bothered me we did not end on good terms. I knew that the only way I would have closure would be to randomly run into him someday.

“Nothing in this universe occurs by accident.”

—NEALE DONALD WALSCH

That night, I lifted a prayer, asking God to have me run into Andrew while I was on my trip. I had heard a rumor that he'd moved to Colorado but had no idea where he lived geographically. In my prayer, I specifically requested that I run into Andrew "somewhere near here in Denver, like the grocery store, while he's alone, so I can have that closure." Then I laughed to myself and apologized to God for the absurdity of it all.

The next day I had forgotten about this when I volunteered to do the lunch run for my friend's family. I didn't have a vehicle, so I jogged to a place about a mile away. On the way to the restaurant, I stopped to grab some beverages from a grocery store. It was the Fourth of July weekend, and the store was nearly deserted. As I was about to check out, I had the sudden urge to turn around and go to the other side of the store; on the final aisle, there stood Andrew! He was shopping alone, and I began to shake, mostly in shock of the fact that my prayer had been answered so literally and immediately. It turns out Andrew had recently moved to the neighborhood near the hospital. We were able to have a good conversation, and I got the closure I had not even realized I needed.

This was one of the few times in my life when I laid out such a specific request in prayer. I am continually amazed by God's love and presence. In a time where my faith was shaken to its core with stress and difficult circumstances, God reminded me He is with me and that I matter to Him. Most importantly, I rejoiced as my friend made a full recovery, and her cancer is now in remission. I'll be the first to admit that I often need things spelled out for me. This literal answer to my prayers still gives me chills; whenever I struggle to feel connected, I remind myself of this example of His goodness and the importance of asking for things instead of trying to go it alone. I believe He knows everything about us; He knows exactly what we need and when we need it. I will forever be grateful for this divine experience.

# As Life Unfolds

**NATHAN JONES**

When I was just a young boy, I was plucked from a normal, traditional life to a hot and smelly foreign land. My parents had begun their careers as overseas teachers and, on the whim of a mid-life crisis, sprang from the safe, homogenous midwestern life to find adventure in Lahore, Pakistan. While transformational and instructive, challenging and illuminating, our ten months there were plenty of an overseas experience for me. After ten months, we returned home to the safe and easy life of middle America, and I had no intention of further change. But for my parents, Pakistan was the spark that ignited their fire and a fifteen-year overseas career. After another year in Minnesota, my parents sat me down to tell me they had been offered jobs in Brazil, and we would be moving there in August. While I should have been excited—Brazil is basically the opposite of Pakistan—I was very much against another foreign endeavor. Likely anticipating my disdain for this news, my parents presented an olive branch. They offered that we relocate to Colorado when we returned in the summer.

I had traveled around the country a fair bit by this point, and it seemed like the cool people had Colorado plates. You know, those Subaru-driving, bike- or boat-toting, Patagonia-wearing, athletic folk. And of course, the few times I had been through Colorado, I thoroughly enjoyed it. The cool mountain air, the aspen forests, the beautiful vistas, the tall mountains—yes, the mountains were where I belonged. By this time, with college beginning to enter the back of my mind, I had made it clear that Colorado's higher education institutions were at the top of my list! And so, my parents, with finances at the top of their minds, thought in-state tuition seemed a better option than out-of-state. With reluctance, but an understanding that I didn't have any choice, I accepted the terms of their deal. That summer, we set off on a road trip to Colorado, intent on finding our summer home.

Our target was Montrose, Colorado. A town that appeared to be small but growing, unassuming but full of potential. As it turns out, Montrose is hot and dry. Too hot and dry for us, so we started the long drive home. Before leaving the state, we took a rafting trip down the Taylor River, just north of Gunnison. Maybe my parents wanted to appease me since they figured they were not going to find the perfect summer home, and we were about to return to Minnesota with that as our permanent summer base.

After the raft trip, the fastest route to the central plains and the highways that would lead us back to the mosquito feeding grounds of the upper Midwest was via Taylor Park and Cottonwood Pass. As we descended towards the valley below, we began to realize we had stumbled upon a real gem. We rolled into Buena Vista, impressed by the natural beauty, small size, quaint streets, and proximity to mountains. This was where we wanted to live! My parents chatted as we approached what was then the only stoplight in town. They agreed that if a realtor's office were open, they would stop, but if not, we would continue on our way. It was July Fourth—what businesses would be open?

Back in that day, there was a real estate office right on the corner by the only stoplight. And wouldn't you believe it, it was open! We parked the car, and all walked in just in time as they were about to close up for the day so they could watch the parade. But my parents and the realtor made plans to meet the next afternoon to have a look around. From there, we continued with our plans and ended up camping among the rustling aspens below the 14ers. The next morning, on my birthday, we hiked up Mount Belford. It was my first 14er! We got an early start and got up to the summit and back down quickly so that we could meet the realtor. Looking at houses and land was a blur for me, but eventually, we found a small parcel of land north of town. My parents made an offer that day, and the land was soon ours. But because we had so much to prepare for our trip to Brazil, we made the trek back to Minnesota.

“Sometimes home has a heartbeat.”

—BEAU TAPLIN

Two summers later, I was playing pickup soccer on the town field in Buena Vista. Our log home was being built, my grandparents were moving out to be closer to us—their only daughter and only grandchild. I had just made the difficult decision to finish high school in Buena Vista instead of going with my parents to Seoul, South Korea. Among the group of kids and young adults playing soccer was a cute girl with blond hair and nice strong legs. She was kind and friendly, but a little shy, and she was a very good soccer player! Being a shy kid myself, I didn't dare speak to this girl! That fall, as I enrolled in classes at the high school, the counselor suggested that I meet a girl to help with the transition to a new school. She said this girl and I had lots of similarities. She was the biology teacher's daughter, she liked being outdoors, and she loved soccer. Of course, being as shy as I was, I didn't make that connection as suggested. But soon enough, I met that girl in class. While it wasn't love at first sight, that girl made an impression on me, and the next year, while I was a freshman at college in Gunnison, Colorado—only an hour and a half drive away—we started dating. That was eighteen years ago, and today we have been married for eleven years and have an amazing little boy. Now we live just two miles from the soccer field where we first met.

Had any small detail of that summer road trip to Colorado been different, we may not have passed through Buena Vista. Had we known about the many other small mountain towns where we could have ended up, we might have chosen one of them. Had we decided to go rafting on any other river, we might not have driven over Cottonwood Pass. Had that realty office not been open, we might not have bought land in Buena Vista. Had I decided to go with my parents and finish high school in South Korea, I would have never set foot in Buena Vista High School. Had any of these things been different, I would never have met the love of my life!

*Chapter Two*

# Divine Intervention

# Angelic Messengers on the Road

As soon as I received word, I was on the road from Colorado to Albuquerque, New Mexico. My brother's son had just been born and diagnosed with Down Syndrome and would be undergoing several surgeries. I arrived at the hospital to find my sister-in-law holding her beautiful baby. The tubes that were attached to Michael, and all the beeps of monitors, returned me to the neonatal trauma I experienced with the birth of my son; I had not been in a neonatal unit for years. But I pushed those feelings away to be present for my brother and his wife and two daughters as they were processing the immediate medical needs of their newborn. Michael was exceptionally beautiful. Were those almond eyes, really? Did he really have a heart defect? What was this talk of esophageal surgery? Reality, disbelief, and concern were all wrapped into one big tangle of emotions for all of us. We stayed at the hospital for hours and then joined family members at my brother's home to discuss, cry, and hug. We had a lot to learn about Down Syndrome, and we would learn together.

Those two days became a blur; I offered the best I could and headed back to Colorado. Alone in my car, I could finally let go of the emotions I had suppressed, and I cried.

Then I saw them.

A young family of four appeared to be stranded along the highway. Two small children were huddled in front of their mother, who was trying to protect them from the wind and fast-moving cars. I had to help. I drove to the next exit and turned around. It was several miles before I arrived at the next exit that would lead me back to them.

I finally pulled over, approaching the family cautiously. "Can I help?" I asked. There was something very surreal and beautiful about the family. I couldn't name it. But for some reason, the children seemed ethereal; the parents projected a soothing calm that relaxed me. The man said, "Yes, you can. Would you mind driving my wife and children to Santa Fe and dropping them off at a hotel there? I'll stay here and wait for the tow truck."

We piled into the car, and as I began driving, I explained I was an elementary school teacher and had just spent the weekend with my brother and his family. My heart poured open regarding the birth of their son. The woman politely listened and then said, "I am actually a Special Education teacher. In fact, my best friend has Down Syndrome. He was raised by an Episcopal priest and his wife. One day my friend asked me, 'Do you know the best thing about having Down Syndrome?' And then he told me it was because he just lives one day to the next and never worries about anything."

With a few deep breaths, I blinked away tears to turn my attention to the darling children until we arrived at their destination. I dropped the family off and continued the long drive ahead. As I listened to the radio, an ad came on. There was going to be a special talk show about Down Syndrome the next night.

"Oh, my gosh," I thought. "I can't wait to tell my brother about this trip home. He will never believe it." That was twenty-two years ago. My nephew has been a blessing to our family. He is full of love and life. He has a sense of humor and loves to dance. Best of all, he has a heart of gold, is adored by his family and friends, and happily lives one day at a time.

“This is a brief life, but in its brevity, it offers us some splendid moments, some meaningful adventures.”

—RUDYARD KIPLING

# It Is Not Your Time

CARYL WALLIN

I was living alone on Vancouver Island during an incredibly difficult time in my life. I had experienced a series of losses over a two-year period. My parents had divorced after over thirty years of marriage and six children, I had ended a tumultuous eight-year relationship with my boyfriend, and my grandmother for whom I had been named had died. These personal losses were difficult, but the final straw was when my precious two-year-old golden retriever puppy died after ingesting something on the beach of our new home on the island. I was devastated.

I became very depressed, and my senses numbed. The surrounding area was unbelievably beautiful, but I could no longer feel the beauty. In fact, my sadness overcame all other emotions. But I was aware enough to have this concern me. One day as I was driving along a lonely road and looking up to the sky, I began sobbing, "Please let me come home." But the answer that came to me was loud and clear. "NO! It is not the time."

It was then I knew I had to do something. Exploring options, I decided to enroll in a dream class. Throughout the course, I began having the most amazing and vivid dreams. A turning point for me was one dream that was particularly life-changing:

*I was standing in a room on top of an extremely high building. The windows on all sides of the room stretched from the floor to the ceiling. I looked out the windows into the dark night sky that was filled with a multitude of bright stars. The most amazing feeling of intense love and comfort came over me. I felt as if I was surrounded by the most indescribable joy and all-encompassing love. When I awoke the next morning, the feeling remained with me. It was a very vivid and palpable feeling that gave me a strong sense that everything would be okay.*

That was thirty-one years ago. Because of this experience, I have learned gratitude and deep appreciation for this wonderful life. It was truly not the time for me "to go home."

> "She said she cried at least once a day. Not because she was sad, but because the world was so beautiful and life was so short."
>
> —BRIAN ANDREAS

# For Ed

GAIL BINDER

I was only fifty-five when I was hospitalized with a blood clot in my lung. I had been short of breath for a week, and when I reached the point of being unable to climb the flight of stairs in my house, I became alarmed. My regular doctor was out of town, so I had been procrastinating on calling for an appointment. But something was obviously wrong.

After a scope, I was hospitalized immediately and placed on a blood thinner. My doctor told me how serious a pulmonary embolism can be.

My husband, Bob, of thirty years, and I had divorced several years earlier, and both of us had remarried. My second husband, Ed, had lost his wife, Gigi, to heart disease two years before we married. But with both Bob and Ed having served as colonels in the Air Force, we were all well-acquainted with one another from serving on military bases at the same time. In fact, the four of us were friends, and after my divorce from Bob, we remained friends.

Ed was very much in love with Gigi, and the loss of her had been hard on him. When Ed and I reconnected after he had heard Bob and I were divorced, the new life we chose to build together was special. Ed treated me with great kindness and love. We traveled the world together but also enjoyed leisurely mornings of coffee and crossword puzzles.

I thought of these things as I lay in the hospital room. One night I was feeling incredibly sad about the situation. But it was more of sadness for Ed. I began to pray. I prayed that if it were my time to go, I would accept that.

But I also prayed for more time because I did not want Ed to suffer the loss of two wives.

My eyes were closed as I prayed, but I saw a very bright light. I opened my eyes, but the room was dark. When I closed my eyes again, there was the same bright white light. I opened my eyes again, and this time the light was in front of me. It was an angel saying, "You will be alright."

But more than what I saw was what I felt in that moment. I was no longer afraid. I felt a deep sense of love, warmth, and comfort.

It was like I was being held.

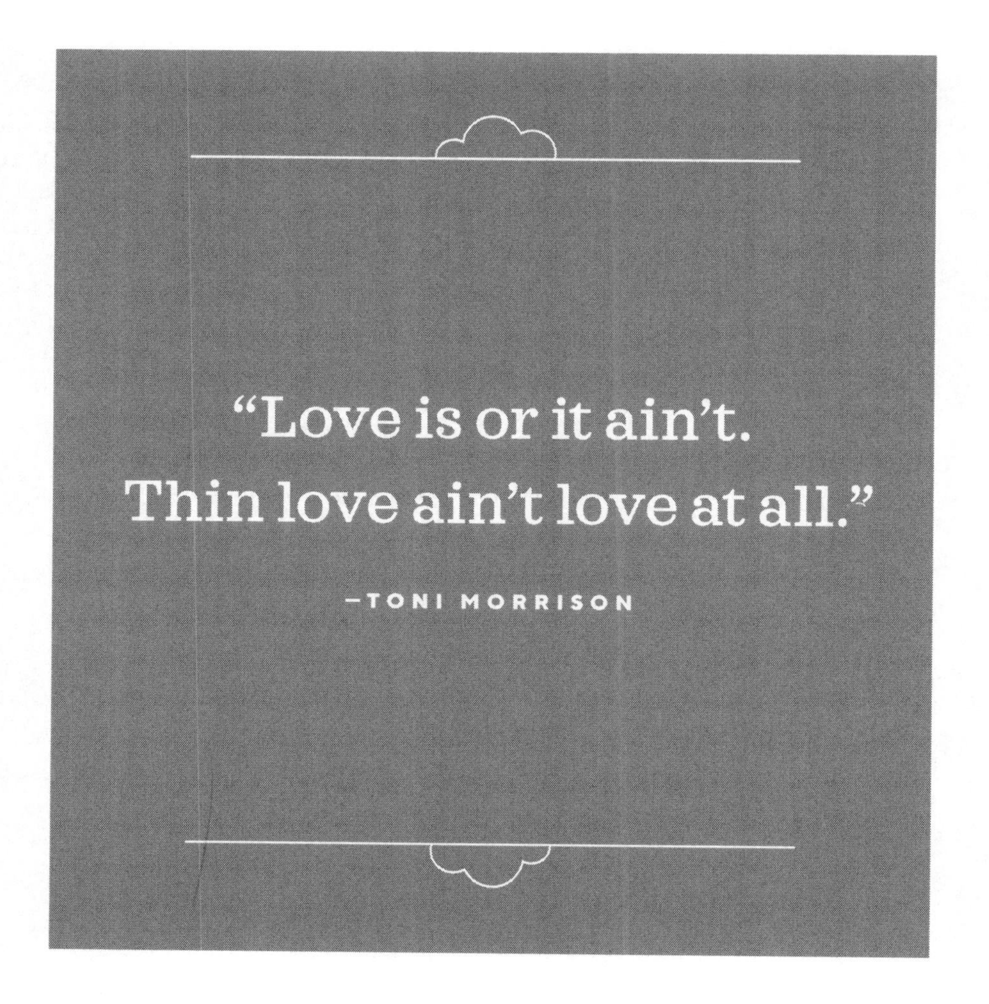

"Love is or it ain't.
Thin love ain't love at all."
–TONI MORRISON

# Coming to My Aid

When I was seven years old, I was riding my bicycle. It was slightly too large for me, and I had not yet mastered great control. I was biking alone on the sidewalk in front of our apartment building. Cars were parked inward, facing the curb of the sidewalk. Before I knew what was happening, my bicycle tumbled off the pavement into the small space between a parked car and the sidewalk. There was just enough space for me to fall between the fender of the car and the curb of the sidewalk. When I lost control, my bicycle went over the curb and the bicycle fell on top of me. I recall screaming as I was pinned and tried desperately to push off the bicycle. It was useless for I was small, and I was pinned by this bicycle that was too large for me. I don't recall seeing anyone or hearing anyone speak, but I do recall the moment the bicycle was lifted off me and clambering my way onto the sidewalk. I vaguely recall seeing a shadowy figure walking away. The figure appeared to glance at me for a moment, but when I looked again, the figure was gone. I had pain in my thigh, and I limped up the sidewalk, pushing my bicycle to my apartment building. I collapsed against my mother, sobbing, trying to convey to her what had happened. I was more shaken than injured but was left perplexed by the nagging question, "Who or what helped me?"

“The only source of knowledge is experience.”

—ALBERT EINSTEIN

# The Timely Package

My grandmother became pregnant with my father during the Great Depression.

"Not now," my grandmother recalled feeling. "How will we ever manage?"

Work for my grandfather was scarce, and food was being rationed.

My grandmother became quite depressed at the increasingly dire circumstances after my father was born. One winter day, she had reached the end of her hope that things would ever improve. She planned to go to the garage with her six-month-old son Skippy, start the car, and leave the door closed. "We will just go to sleep and not wake up," she thought. She thought it would be the only way to escape the harsh realities of the poverty they were facing.

In her frenzy of creating this plan, there was a knock at the door. The mailman placed a package in her arms. It was from her sister, who was living in Florida.

She opened the package and held up a snowsuit for her little baby.

"I hope this helps Skippy stay warm this winter," the note read.

My grandmother held the snowsuit to her chest and looked at her precious child. It stirred her out of the dreadful fantasy she had played out in her mind. She knew then that everything was going to be alright. And it was. Her son grew into a remarkable young man, married his high school sweetheart, had six children, and served an honorable thirty-year career in the Air Force.

“The tragic consequences of life can be overcome by the magical strength that resides in the human heart.”

—RUDOLFO ANAYA

# A Tap

LAURA REIS

When I was in the eighth grade, I was watching an indoor racquetball game from the second floor, looking down over the court from the edge of a wall. I was learning to play tennis that year and enjoyed spending my free time at the tennis and racquetball club.

As I watched the game below, I was leaning a bit over the edge of the wall when I felt someone deliberately tap me on my shoulder. Assuming it was one of my other friends, I turned my head to look. No one was there. I quickly looked the other way. There was not a soul around. I darted over to the steps leading down to the main walkway in the gym, and I still saw no one. As I stepped back up to the viewing area, a ball came flying up just where I had been standing. That instantly gave me chills.

I will never forget that tapping sensation on my shoulder. It was a firm and deliberate tap, tap, tap. But I also realized later that moment had saved me from getting hit in the face with the ball. It may have also served as a warning to not lean so far over the wall. As I shared my story with others, it was suggested to me that it was my guardian angel tapping on my shoulder. That is what I believe now, too.

“Take care of this moment.”

—MAHATMA GANDHI

# The Singed Cord

Like Laura's experience in her short story "A Tap," I had what appears to be in hindsight an experience with Divine intervention. One day I was drying my hair with a hair dryer. No one else was in the house, yet over the dryer, I heard my name being called. I turned off the dryer and listened and called out, "Yes? Hello? I'm here. Did someone call me?" I walked around the house, and it reaffirmed what I knew; no one was home. I went back to my hairdryer, and it would not turn on. I looked closely at the cord and discovered it had shorted out. A small, singed spot was on the end of the cord.

“Be still. The quieter you become, the more you hear.”

—RAM DASS

# In the Nick of Time

STEVEN LIEBOWITZ

In August of 2012, I took a road trip with my wife, Jenny, from Colorado Springs, Colorado, to Santa Fe, New Mexico, for the Labor Day Fiesta. After an uneventful six-hour drive, we arrived at our hotel. Upon entering the hotel lobby, I asked Jenny to check us in, as I had to use the little boys' room. Feeling completely fine, I entered the restroom to offboard the morning coffee and sodas consumed during the drive. I was standing in the bathroom, not a care in the world, when out of the blue, I felt a stabbing pain in my abdomen. The pain was so intense I started to vomit uncontrollably. I managed to stumble into the lobby and told Jenny to get me to a hospital. Luckily, the hotel clerk advised the hospital was just up the street.

Within minutes, Jenny pulled into the emergency entrance of St. Vincent's Hospital, where emergency personnel immediately transferred me to a trauma room for examination. The intense pain remained and increased in intensity throughout what seemed an eternity. After numerous tests, the hospital's trauma surgeon advised us that my colon had ruptured and I would require emergency surgery, or I would die. In the span of sixty minutes, I went from a happy, healthy man with no symptoms to a man withering in intense pain facing life or death surgery. I couldn't sign the consent form quickly enough.

I do not remember my first week after surgery but recall vivid memories of what I would define as an out-of-body experience. I remember being in the

“A brush with death always helps us to live our lives better.”

—PAULO COEHLO

surgical operating room and briefly seeing myself on the table surrounded by the medical team. My father passed away in 2006, yet in this experience, I met Dad and was having a discussion with him. Immediately thereafter, I was walking alone outside in a gorgeous countryside. There were also large, beautiful white buildings with columns. The colors of the area I saw were so vibrant, like nothing I have ever seen on earth. Although I could not see anyone, I heard the most calming, ethereal music emanating around me. I had no pain, no worries, and I felt totally at peace.

The first memory I had after the surgery was of familiar voices and feeling intense abdominal pain from the seventeen-inch-long incision held together by fifty-seven staples. I opened my eyes, saw my family gathered in my room, and heard them discussing my room layout and the location of the television. Apparently, the room was a single patient room that was so small no one could figure out how to place the bed in a location where the television could be used. It was then I started having a conversation with my dad. My dad asked me how I was feeling and told me I was going to be okay. My dad then told me how to position the bed in the room for maximum efficiency. I told my family that my dad was there and what he recommended. Later, I also told my wife about what I had experienced; it was what I believed to be my visit to heaven.

# A Three-Year Old's Angel Encounter

One afternoon when my three-year-old son was napping, I flipped through television talk shows. Watching afternoon television was uncharacteristic of me, as I would usually exercise, read, or rest. However, I felt compelled this day to turn my attention to a show that captured my interest.

A discussion was in progress with adults who, as young children, had near-death experiences. I was interested because our son had become extremely ill at birth and spent a week on a ventilator, two more weeks in intensive care after the ventilator was removed, and six months on oxygen at home. At the end of six months, he turned the corner and made a complete and remarkable recovery. He was considered a "miracle baby" by many, and after his recovery, the doctors indicated they were amazed he had pulled through the mystery illness.

As I listened to the conversation on this television program, I became more skeptical as the discussion turned to "guardian angels." While I had heard of this phenomenon, I believed they were a trendy pursuit of comfort for the human spirit. Nonetheless, I continued lending a curious and somewhat sympathetic ear, but by the end of the show, I flipped off the television without any further contemplation on the matter.

About a month later, as my son was awakening from a nap, we were playing with a stuffed animal that was given to him as a newborn in the hospital. I told him how nice everyone had been to give him presents. He said, "I liked the doctors and nurses." I agreed and said he was so well cared for by so many people. Then he said, "I liked the one with the fairy wings."

I gasped. My mind immediately flashed back to the television talk show. I was in disbelief. Then to be sure, I asked my son, "Do you mean the doctors and nurses?" He answered, matter-of-factly, "The lady with the fairy wings was nice." We had never read books about fairies or angels, so I could make no connection to anything he may have heard previously. I could only believe he had an angelic experience in the hospital.

Later I relayed the story to a friend, and she as well, responded matter-of-factly, "I wonder who his guardian angel is."

When it is out of the mouths of babes, how can one deny the possibilities?

*This account by Kathleene Keidel was published in God's Vitamin "C" for the Spirit of Women, compiled by Kathy Collard Miller. Starburst Publisher, Inc. 1997.*

“Life can only be understood backwards, but it must be lived forward.”

—SOREN KIERKEGAARD

# Close Call

**ROSIE FEDORA**

There was nothing else I could do, so I lay there exhausted. An odd rhythm filled my chest. "Can you feel that?" came the query, the doctor's eyes darting back and forth from the monitor to my face and back again. "Unbelievable," he said and quickly left the room.

Yes, I felt it, an unsurmountable wave of chaos, as if two sumo wrestlers had taken over my chest. Yet, I had walked into the emergency room just minutes ago, and in a half-whisper, calmly told the ER registrar, "I think I am having a heart emergency."

I had told my family the day before, "I'm fine. I'll go to the ER in the morning." But later that night, I was in eminent danger. Alone and unable to move from my bed, an explosive irregular heart rhythm took over. Yes, I had waited too long. Over the next forty-eight hours at the hospital, the IV's slow drip kept my blood pressure from dangerously dropping. No one knew why I had developed a life-threatening heart arrhythmia unresponsive to medication other than emergency drugs; I learned I was in heart failure.

Only in retrospect can I see the denial I was in, the months of close calls passing out momentarily while driving, along with an increasing sense of free-floating anxiety that encircled my life. When a friend said that I may have died the night before entering the hospital, I could not deny it. In truth, I had felt the irregular heartbeat but never told anyone. The moment I knew I

"The thing is to understand myself: the thing is to find a truth which is true for me, to find the idea for which I can live and die. That is what I now recognize as the most important thing."

—SOREN KIERKEGAARD

was having an emergency, I sat in fear over the side of the bed, afraid I would not see another day, and I prayed.

I called out, "Jesus, where are you?"

The silence and darkness seemed to echo through time's cavernous walls, yet I continued to call out again and again. Suddenly, the darkness opened to a space of endless dimension and light. Jesus turned to me. He first looked directly at me, then gazed past me. When He raised His hand, I found myself back in my room. Sitting on the side of the bed, I was greeted by luminous beings. I felt their presence and was reassured they were there to guide me and help me. I felt an immediate deep peace come over me. The last thing I remember is hearing heavenly music and feeling the regular beating of my heart. I fell fast asleep.

I called my sister the next morning for a ride to the ER. Despite the return of my irregular heartbeat, I felt confident I would make it to the ER in time. Once admitted, I felt a deep sense of reassurance as I knew things were enfolding as they should. The doctor, fascinated by the fact I was still conscious and talking, decided to do heart surgery to investigate my chaotic heartbeat. When I awoke after four hours of rather complicated surgery, I felt a sense of elation. My regular heartbeat had returned. I learned that fifty-two spots in my upper left atrium had been ablated (removed), each potentially triggering an irregular heartbeat.

The face of Jesus Christ is as alive to me today as it was that night. To this day, I remind people to ask for help. I believe we are not alone.

# Alone, But Not Alone

My son was born by emergency cesarean in a rural hospital and within hours was hospitalized with an unspecified illness. My husband and I followed the ambulance to the hospital in the city ninety miles away. Within hours, he was in the Neonatal Intensive Care Unit. Every day was met with uncertainty but also with love and compassion by all the medical staff. Within twenty-four hours, I began running a fever myself, and after five days of uterine pain and high fever, I saw a doctor who hospitalized me with a raging infection caused by a large uterine abscess. I was placed in a room two floors above my son. My doctor put me on three IV antibiotics, but after two days, there was no improvement. I was told the doctors would be doing a needle aspiration procedure to try to remove the infection from the abscess. Surgery would be a risky last resort as a ruptured abscess would be life-threatening.

The night before the procedure, and after my husband and three-year-old daughter came for a short visit, I was left alone in my room. Fever and fear of the impending procedure caused me to shiver. I pulled up the blankets around my chin and folded my hands, closed my eyes, and began to pray. I said, "I accept whatever is in your will, Lord; please take care of my husband and children. Thank you so much for my family and my life."

Suddenly, I felt the most incredible warmth flow over me. An all-encompassing feeling of love filled the room, and I no longer felt alone. The presence of Divine love created a calming sense of peace in me. At that moment, no matter the outcome, I knew everything would be okay.

The next morning my mother walked into my hospital room unexpectedly.

"Mom! What are you doing here?"

She looked perplexed. "I don't know. I could not sleep last night. I just felt you should not be alone." She stayed with me until it was time for the procedure. As I was wheeled away, I thanked her for coming.

In the treatment room, two doctors tried unsuccessfully to remove the thick toxin from the abscess. "We will give it one more day, but we may have to do the surgery tomorrow," my doctor warned. During this time of uncertainty, I felt myself *accept*.

The next morning, my doctor looked at my chart and held it up into the air with his hands overhead, "Hallelujah! Your fever has broken! No surgery! We will keep you here a few more days on the antibiotics, but you have turned the corner." Within twenty-four hours, I could visit my newborn son again, both of us wired to IV tubes.

One afternoon a nurse I had never seen came to my room. She told me she had heard about my case and presented me with a gift basket for both my son and me. She didn't tell me her name; I later tried to find out who she was so I could thank her. No one had any idea, and I never saw her again. I was discharged shortly thereafter, and my son was discharged two weeks later. Within six months, we had both fully recovered from our illnesses. I will always remember the love, kindness, and compassion extended to us both by the staff, and I remain eternally grateful to the Spirit of LOVE that was present.

"Love is the bridge
between you
and everything."

—RUMI

*Chapter Three*

# After Death Encounters

# Personal Account of Grieving

T.T. KARLSSON

Cremation is an option for many people who have lost a loved one. The issue of what to do with the cremains and where to put them can be an overwhelming experience. I was certain that it was appropriate to place my daughter's ashes in her room in a cabinet, where she could be comfortable, safe, and secure. Her friends from college came to sit on her bed, lounge in her room, grieve, and reminisce. Comfortable, safe, secure.

A day or two later as I walked down the hall to her bedroom to check on her, I noticed something just a little off. Right before opening the door I smelled something. And then it hit me. As I entered the room I was engulfed by the smell of smoke. It was like some smoldering campfire had been burning all night.

There was a haze of smoke carried by bands of dry mist, as if there were several strands and layers of tiny cirrus clouds filling the upper half of the room. Thin wisps of whitish gray smoke hung in the air, moving ever so slowly. My daughter was truly angry.

My mistake was undeniable. Apologizing profusely, I moved her to the closet. No luck. Finally, I took her urn to a closet in the middle of the house. That did the trick. By the next morning, the smoke had disappeared, and the little wispy clouds were gone. I don't know why it happened this way, but it was unmistakably real.

Today, we live in a different house a long way from where we were before. My daughter sits on the top of my closet, where she is supposed to be.

"'Thin places,' the Celts called this space, both seen and unseen, where the door between the world and the next is cracked open for a moment, and the light is not all on the other side. God shaped space. Holy."

—REV. SHARLANDE SLEDGE

# The Bonanza

**BARBARA RUIZ**

My dad lived a long life. He had always been full of curiosity and pursued many hobbies and interests, from exploring pioneer ghost towns to writing textbooks about computers. When he learned he had cancer, he fought it for twenty-three years; he enthusiastically kept living, especially persisting with one of his favorite pastimes—flying small airplanes as a private pilot. In his later years, he had retired from flying Bonanza airplanes, fast, powerful vehicles that took my sister and parents and me on many family vacations years before. Though he continued to fly smaller, less expensive aircraft, we always had a special place in our hearts and memories for the sleek shape and distinctive V-shaped tails of Bonanzas.

Dad died at home with family by his side. The night following his passing, we cleared the room of hospital supplies, transporting load after load to the barn where they would be stored until hospice could pick them up. Returning to the house after removing the final items, I looked up at the cold, clear January night sky. A full moon brilliantly illuminated the clouds and an airplane contrail that pierced right through the lunar light. I encouraged everybody to look up and suggested that it might be a sign Dad was on his way to new adventures. As soon as all my siblings and Mom were focused on the sight, a small plane with a V-tail flew right through the contrail and the full moon. It was a Bonanza. If I had seen this alone, I would have questioned my eyes, but since we all experienced this phenomenon, we are inclined to embrace it and be thankful for Dad's final farewell.

"Listen to the silence to hear the heartbeat of the universe."

—LAWRENCE OVERMIRE

# First Dream After Departure

**MARGERY DORFMEISTER**

My beloved hubby of sixty-five years died on April 30, 2015. While John was alive, I often had nightmares that we got separated somewhere, and I could not find my way back to where he had dropped me off and where I had promised to meet him. Strangely, the setting was often a familiar location: Chicago, where he was born; the north side of Madison, Wisconsin, where we raised our children; Los Angeles, where we frequently visited my maiden aunt Dorothy; or the campus of Ripon College, where we dated before becoming engaged.

In my dream, I would be in agony trying to reach him. The city streets would become muddy lanes. The familiar stores and houses would morph into weird castles and rock walls. The streetlights would go out. I would seek out the Sears store in Madison or the Commons on the Ripon campus, but when I got inside, there was no way out. One room just opened into another, and the people in the stores were rude to me for disturbing them. Worst of all, I was weighted down with so much baggage in my arms that it was hard to move. One by one, I seemed to lose my belongings. I lost my purse and ID, my packages, my hat, coat, and gloves until I was down to one tiny nightie. When I woke up, I would be tangled up in the bedding, and John would be mumbling, "You were talking in your sleep again."

Now all these years later, following his death, I would be alone in my bedroom waiting for some sign from him. A friend of mine had dreamed more than once that her deceased husband appeared to her, acknowledging her from a distance. He was waiting next to his parked car, but they were unable to reach each other. I was curious to know what my first meeting with John would be like. And then I had the dream that gave me the answer:

*I was at a seaside resort with our two children. Our daughter, Peggy, was about four, and our son, Paul, was seven. We had been at the beach, and Peggy put up a fuss when I said we had to leave to go inside the hotel. It was getting close to bedtime for the children. I tucked the two of them in, and after they were asleep, I left them to go to another room in the hotel to attend a seminar. A short time later, I returned to the room to check on the children, but when I got there, Peggy was missing. I was frantic and woke up Paul to ask him where she was, but he had no idea. He fell back to sleep, and I left the room again to search for her. I was riddled with guilt for leaving them alone. On my way down the first-floor hall to the back door, I passed the indoor swimming pool. I looked through the glass door and saw there were people inside. I opened the door and went in. There right at the end of the pool was John, sitting on a bench, his back against the wall. He was wearing a white shirt and white pants—an outfit I had never seen him wear when he was living. He beckoned to me reassuringly and pointed to a small rubber raft in the pool where a lifeguard was giving a demonstration of life-saving equipment. My little girl was asleep at the bottom of the raft, all safe and sound. I was more than relieved to know that her daddy was looking after her, just like he had done in his life.*

“When one has
a grateful heart,
life is so beautiful.”

—ROY T. BENNETT

# They Sent Messages

On several occasions, I have heard voices from deceased love ones. They came with messages.

* One night, as I was drifting to sleep, months after my best friend had died, I took a moment and said, "Connie, I miss you." I heard her voice, clear as a bell, say, "Hey there, Kathy. It is so beautiful here. You just can't imagine how beautiful it is."

* A recent high school graduate died in a tragic automobile accident. The community held a candlelight vigil for her; we sang songs and honored her, mourned her loss. The next night, just as I was falling asleep, I distinctly heard her voice. "Hey, Mrs. K. Can you please tell my parents I love them? And tell Mr. K. hello for me." She sounded so happy and cheerful, like the young woman I remembered her to be.

* Another friend lost her husband unexpectedly after a night of musical jamming with friends. They played their guitars, sang songs, made music into the night. When they returned home, he collapsed of a sudden heart attack and died. My friend had known him since she was twelve years old. He was quite a few years older than she, but once she became an adult, they married and had two young children. She was devastated. Her husband appeared to me in a dream and said, "Please tell my family I love them."

“The spiritual life does not remove us from the world but leads us deeper into it.”

—HENRI J. M. NOUWEN

# Everything Will Be Alright

My mother was just two years old when her father died. Her mother was a registered nurse—a stoic and kind-hearted woman. After her husband's death, she worked for an obstetrician, who became a lifelong dear friend to her. My siblings and I loved Dr. King as we were growing up and considered him a grandfather figure to us, hoping someday they would marry. Little did we know there was no romantic interest, just platonic friendship.

Our grandmother was very practical, a no-nonsense woman with strong values and strength. Raising two children as a single mother in the 1930s and 1940s was no easy task. Over the years, I learned to have great respect and admiration for her. When I was on a college break, I spent a weekend with her. She told me more about the grandfather I had never met. He had been a talented athlete in college and played on the rugby team. No one ever suspected he had a heart condition that would lead to heart failure at such an early age. She always blamed herself for not recognizing the symptoms of a heart problem when he wasn't feeling well over the Thanksgiving weekend.

She told me when she was dressing for his funeral, she looked up and suddenly saw him standing before her. Grief can cause great emotional distress, but she said she believed her vision was real. In fact, he spoke to her and said, "Everything will be alright."

I believe my grandmother may have spent the remainder of her life as a single woman because of this vision; she believed they would be reunited. Dr. King perhaps filled a void of male companionship on some level, but he could never replace the man she married.

> "Be watchful. The grace of God appears suddenly. It comes without warning to an open heart."
>
> —RUMI

# Her Final Word

JENNY LIEBOWITZ

I have always wished I had the spiritual gift of receiving messages from the ***other side***. While I have not been so fortunate to have such experiences, I did witness an interesting event.

My mother-in-law was diagnosed with late-stage cancer. She took the news in a very resigned way and declined quickly in a matter of a few weeks. The family gathered around her bed, speaking to her gently, each expressing their farewell with loving words and hoping for a glimpse of a response.

On her last day of life, she suddenly said, "Hi, Kim," without even opening her eyes. Kim was her young daughter who had died at the tender age of six. We all knew she was seeing Kim. She then said, "Hi, Tiki." Tiki was one of the family dogs from many years back. We asked her, "Is Stan (her late husband) there also?" and she smiled and nodded. Everyone was astounded.

However, for me, it was this next display of nature that was so interesting. As my mother-in- law took her last breath, I heard a noise at the window. I looked outside at the onset of a sudden storm. A winter storm was not in the forecast. But the wind blew ferociously, and sleet pounded against the window. My first thought was, "Wow! She really did not want to go." The storm continued all night, and the high winds even ripped our hot tub cover from its buckles. I have always felt this was my mother-in-law's grand exit, making her final statement that she was still with us.

“Spirit is an invisible force made visible in all life.”

—MAYA ANGELOU

# Visitations

MARGERY DORFMEISTER

Three incidents that I considered to be bordering on the supernatural each involved the death of a loved one.

The first had to do with the passing of my grandmother, Lettie Russell, with whom I was close. I had visited her in the hospital after she had suffered a stroke. The prognosis was not good. But the unexpected phenomenon was that I knew immediately when I woke one morning that she had died during the night. I felt her absence keenly before receiving the confirmation.

The second incident was the loss of an early childhood friend, Maxeen, whom I had loved from the time we were three or four years old—living on adjoining farms. She died young, in her mid-sixties, and the day I was told, I went into my home office to work. I am a professional writer —and when I sat down at my typewriter, there was a "presence" in my chair, occupying my space, and I couldn't ease myself back into the seat to settle myself to start work. The space was already occupied, and something was pushing me off the seat. I could not believe what was happening. There was nobody else at home to talk to about it. I just stood up and left the room, walked around a bit, puzzled, of course, and then went back to try to work again. The same thing happened, just as strong as before. I was so upset that I had to abandon work for the day.

Number three occurred when my older sister Fran died. She was my best friend, confidant, and mentor. She was also a writer and helped pave the way for my career. I was full of remorse for her loss. I had already lost my father, then my mother—but losing my dearly beloved sibling, I thought, was unbearable. I was lying on my bed, grieving, when a swoosh of air passed my right shoulder, then moved on down to my feet and out of the bedroom. I felt a great sense of relief as if the grief I had been experiencing was released. It was as though she had come to me to bring the message that, "All will be well." And it was.

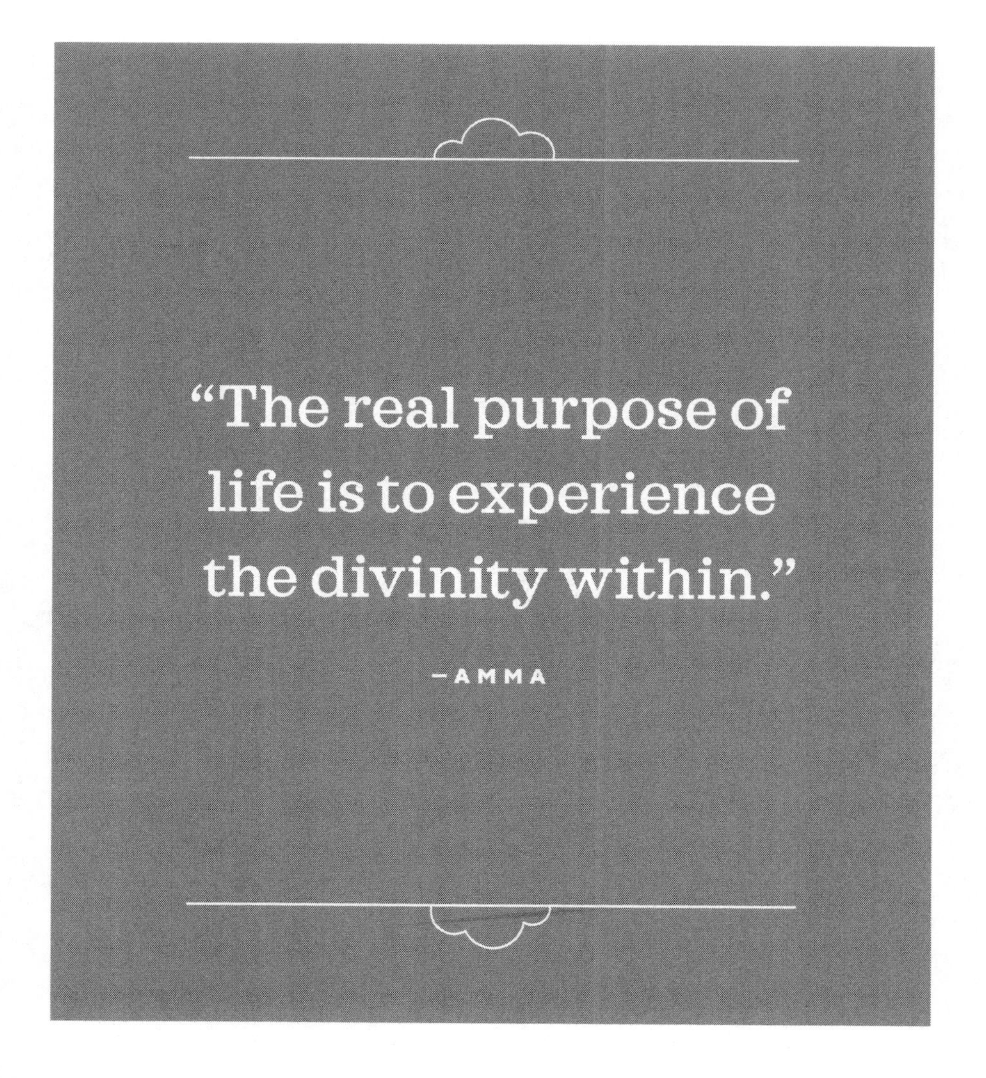

"The real purpose of life is to experience the divinity within."
—AMMA

# Pep

From the time she could stand up and hold on to the sides of her crib, Connie was a force to reckon with. Her parents gave her the pet name, "Pep," as she would bounce up and down in her crib with wild enthusiasm.

Growing up on a farm with seven siblings and a strict but loving father, Connie learned discipline and a work ethic that would serve her well. It also taught her determination and independence and when she was just seventeen, she bicycled from Minnesota to Florida. Alone. She loved riding horses, woodworking, running and hiking, composing songs and singing. Everything she did, she did well and with heart. It was if everything she touched turned to gold.

I met Connie in our junior year of college, and we became fast friends, sharing a home near the college campus with two other roommates. She was a student who settled for nothing less than perfect grades and had a fierce temper when life felt unjust. The day her college professor accused her of plagiarism because the research paper she wrote *in Spanish* for her Spanish class was "too perfect," was the first time I saw the seething anger and tears of injustice. (The professor was unable to prove plagiarism and later apologized.) Connie and I were opposites. She was an extrovert and uninhibited. I was reserved and cautious, on guard. So, the day she danced on the table singing and playing her guitar didn't surprise me. "Come on," she'd laugh and encourage me, but I just watched her in the same way she watched me being the observer.

My reserve intrigued her. Though different we were kindred spirits. The year she traveled to Europe was the beginning of a shared love of corresponding by letters that continued into our adult lives as we married and had children. A lover of languages, Connie was a beloved high school teacher, fluent in Spanish and French (and self-taught in Russian). She left a huge hole in the hearts of all those who knew her and loved her when she died too soon.

Shortly after her death, I met a new friend who had Connie's vibrancy and charm. We quickly became friends. Perhaps because I missed Connie, I wanted to replace her. Subconsciously, I projected Connie's spirit onto her. We enjoyed a sweet friendship until she moved away and we lost touch. It was then my feelings of loss came full circle. I clung to the grief and did not want to let go.

One day I awoke with an urging to visit one of the last places Connie had been before she died. It was in a homestead cabin that her sister, Christy, had converted to a beautiful Bed and Breakfast. When I arrived, I was embraced with so much love by Christy and in awe of how much her teenage daughter resembled Connie. I sat in the rocking chair on the porch where Connie had sat. I imagined her there, with her guitar singing, looking out onto the beautiful green pasture, reflecting on her life, coming to terms with her terminal illness. The three days that I spent there, I felt Connie's spirit. I imagined her voice, her words, her smiles and laughter. But most of all, I heard her voice loud and clear saying, "It's okay to let go. You can leave your grief here in this place I love. Take the memory of our friendship home." And I did. As E.E. Cummings wrote, *"I carry your heart. I carry it in my heart."*

*Chapter Four*

# Lucid Dreaming

# Between the Thin Spaces

Several months after my father died, I had a lucid dream.

*I was in the room by my front door when the door flew open. My father floated into the room. His face was rosy, his eyes were bright blue. He was beaming as he entered but simply passed by me.*

*"Dad! Dad!" I cried out. "Stop! I want to talk to you." But he floated past me, down the hall, and was gone.*

When I became fully awake, I thought, "He is happy. How I wish he could have had that same happiness and peace when he was alive."

It was in the final months of his life that Dad realized he was so loved; he really "got it." He finally understood what we had tried to tell him for so many years; that he was beloved by his family, by his adult children, and his grandchildren even after a divorce that left our mother reeling. We were grateful that in the end, he knew. But I was even more so grateful now to know that he was at peace and genuinely happy.

“Peace will come wherever it is sincerely invited.”

—ALICE WALKER

# "You Are So Brave"

CARYL WALLIN

After my father's death, I had a dream in which I was skiing on the side of a steep mountain with all my five siblings. One by one, each person would ski off the side of the mountain, over the crest of the hill. It appeared to me to be a complete drop-off. But then they would each return to the crest of the hill.

In my dream, because of my fear of heights, I was unable to even approach the side of the hill despite much encouragement from my sisters and brothers. Finally, my youngest brother, Christopher, took me lovingly but firmly by the arm. He guided me into a chairlift seat and said, "Caryl, you can go down the mountain this way."

The chair began to move, and I heard him say from behind, "But whatever you do, don't let go." The chair swiftly hurled forward.

I felt my feet lifting from the ground, and the drop-off was clearly under me now. I was so terrified I wrapped my arms around the bar and clung for my life. There was nothing below me—just empty space.

When the chair came to a landing, I found myself standing upon solid ground. Surprisingly, my mother was there, and she had a wonderful huge smile on her face saying with urgency, "Hurry! Hurry! He is waiting for you."

As I approached some sort of barrier, perhaps like a fence, I saw Dad sitting in a chair. He was surrounded by figures, but I couldn't see their faces. I heard someone say, "No touching allowed. Those are the rules."

In my dream, I felt as though my father and I spoke, but I could not hear or remember the words. What I do remember is the look on his face and the emotion attached to it. It was a look of longing, love, and great happiness at seeing me.

The next thing I knew, I was awake in bed with the words, "That was so brave of you," floating around me.

My first thought was that I had been with Dad and it was so exciting. I felt like my siblings and I had all been summoned by Dad as a final last wish, and I totally expected them each to recall a similar experience. But that was not the case.

As I have reflected on that dream over the years, I have come to realize that being in someone's presence and being seen by them is as powerful as any words could ever be. My soul's desire to see my father was stronger than my fear of the journey there. I will always cherish my last time with Dad.

“Grow spiritually and help others to do so. It is the meaning of life.”

—LEO TOLSTOY

# Serenity

## NANCY WALTERS

In my late twenties, I started graduate studies in English at Colorado University. I was sure that I could juggle evening classes even though my son Jeff was just a year old. The difficulty came when I needed to do research during the day at a local library. Fortunately, I had a friend who also stayed home with a young child, and she agreed to let Jeff have a play date with her child. I used my free afternoon to do research on the history of drama. As I sat in the old library building, I dug deeper into my topic, surrounded by the dusty old stacks of research material, with only a small space to write. I must have nodded off.

I awoke to a silence and clarity that I had never experienced. The air seemed bright around me, the silence complete, my body at rest, my mind filled with wonder. I felt completely still and relaxed, no intrusion of light or noise, just peace, with no sense of worry—only wanting more of that still clarity. If I had merely nodded off due to lack of sleep, I thought I would be more anxious, more worried about needing to leave, but instead my thoughts and movements just flowed, and I held myself in peace. I have never since experienced such absolute clarity and light. I have even practiced both transcendental and Zen meditation—and while I experience relaxation and peace, I have not had that same clarity.

“Who looks outward dreams, who looks inward awakens.”

—CARL JUNG

# The Art of Communication

MARIA WEBER

I sat on the floor next to my computer and told myself I needed a break from wrapping gifts. It was early December. A fire in the woodstove warmed our log home. Outdoors, our Colorado sky shimmered a frosty blue. I stared out the picture window toward Mt. Princeton to clear my mind. I wanted to draw. I had retreated to the carpet, my favorite place to do my art. With a pen in my hand, I gazed at a page of used computer paper, clean side up. The last time I had tried this had been three years earlier.

And so, I began. I rested my hand on the paper and waited. In a second or two, the muscles clamped down, and my hand was madly looping, scribbling, blackening in areas on the page, leaving other areas white. Energy flowed through my arm as this continued. The energy was focused in my right hand, which was out of control or being controlled by a force that I allowed to seize me. I could have stopped it at any moment by raising my hand from the page, but I did not wish to. Never had the energy moved my hand so quickly. I was feeling a rush of love in my heart and excitement in my solar plexus as the scribbling continued for two minutes.

I watched as a picture took form; it was a doodled sketch in black ink, six inches high by eight inches wide. Nothing fancy. It was a body, torso, head, shoulders, arms, and hands. There were eyes, eyebrows, nose, and a smiling mouth. And then the motion stopped. I stared at the sketch in front of me. Who was it? Was it my muse cheering me on? But two days later, it hit me.

It was my mother who had been dead for four years. After her death, I had hoped for a sign from her. But now, I looked at the arms spread wide, greeting me with beckoning fingers. She was reaching out to hug me. "Thanks, Mom," I whispered.

"When you approach intuitive methods with respect, you become open to hearing from your interior channels."

—CAROLYN MUSS

# My Favorite Room

Many years ago, I wrote this little ditty:

*My favorite room is the room I go to when I want to write*
*With pen in hand and clean white paper, my thoughts flow out just right.*
*My favorite room is the room I go to; it has no chair nor bed.*
*My favorite room is the room I go to, right inside my head.*

When I write, I often sit down and let my thoughts flow. Rarely do I edit. Rarely do I hesitate or stumble or over-think what I want to say. I just allow my thoughts to pour out of me. I have often felt the words were formed in my head long ago, and all I had to do was allow my pen to go with the flow. It is as if a vessel is pouring the words onto the paper. When I sit down to write, there is almost no conscious effort about the process. It is a beautiful feeling. There are times different voices pour out, depending on my mood or the atmosphere, or the inspiration for writing. Some voices I love, and I say to myself, "Ah, there it is. The voice I love."

If I write a card or need to write a poem for a special occasion, I may think about it for a few days. It is like pouring paint onto a piece of paper and watching the colors swirl around until a form begins to take shape. Or it is like the clouds in the sky, Shapeshifters, that create various images that can be named but then morph into something else. This swirling around process may take a day, a week, or even a month, until the moment I am "ready." When that moment comes, I am just the vehicle for those thoughts and words to take form on paper. I sometimes use paper; at other times, I use the keyboard on my computer. A handy notebook or scraps of paper do fine, too.

I once heard the quote, *"I write because there is too much for me to think alone."* I love that quote and identify with it in many ways. Writing is a process of sharing with others who may relate, but it's also allowing the feelings, words, and thoughts in one's head to have a voice.

"We are not human beings having a spiritual experience, we are spiritual beings having a human experience."

—PIERRE TEILHARD DE CHARDIN

# Fire, Then Calm

Thirty years ago, I had a powerful dream.

*I was dressed in white, sitting on a white pedestal, in a white room. All around me flames burned. I held a photograph of my family to my heart, facing the impending doom. Then, the fire was gone, and I found myself walking through a beautiful, lush green lawn. The vivid color was beyond words. I approached a tall, red-brick building, and as I stood next to it, the top of the building was out of view. Yet, I heard music. Seeking the source, I looked up at an open window. The music flowing from the window was so serene, so beautiful. I can only describe it as celestial. It took my breath away, and I kept saying, "Oh, it is so beautiful! So beautiful!"*

When I woke up, I wrote down my dream. The memory of the vibrant colors and ethereal music has stayed with me to this day.

“God comes to us disguised as our life.”

—RICHARD ROHR

# Holding Dad

As my father was dying, my five siblings and I were flying in from various parts of the country to be at his bedside. My flight was scheduled for two days out when my sister called me and said, "Come now." I quickly changed my plans and prepared to leave the next morning. That night I had a dream.

*I was at my father's bedside, holding his hand and telling him everything was going to be okay. I proceeded to name the loved ones who had passed before him, and that he would soon be reunited with them. When I said, "And you'll see your mother," he rolled his eyes at me as if to say, "Thanks for reminding me of that," for though they loved each other, they had a somewhat cantankerous relationship. I pulled him close to me and cradled him on my shoulder, like a small child, and then gently laid him back onto his pillow.*

I woke up to my phone ringing.

"He's gone," my sister was saying.

"I know," I said. "I was with him last night. It was a dream, but it felt so real. I'll be there by evening."

After I arrived and reunited with my siblings, they told me how they had gathered around our father in those final hours. They said it was a beautiful moment when the sun came streaming into the hospital window, and the beams of light fell onto his face. They said he looked very peaceful as he drew his final breath. When they told me the hour that this happened, I did the math and realized it happened when I was dreaming. I believed that my soul was with him, and we had our final goodbyes in this sacred space.

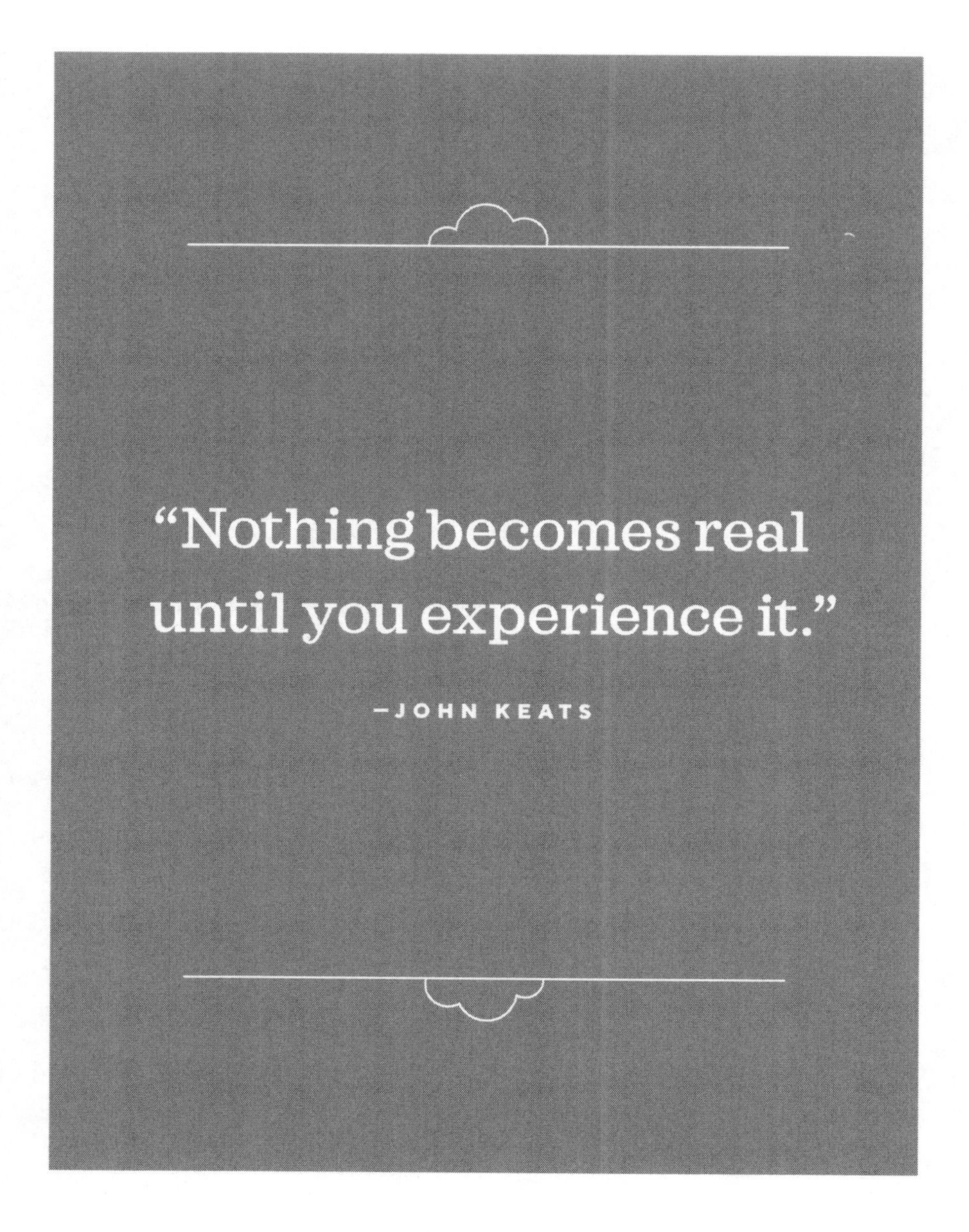

"Nothing becomes real until you experience it."
—JOHN KEATS

# The Seven

*They were there waiting, all seven of them. In white flowing gowns, with misty velour air swirling around them in auras of lavender, rosy-pink, pale yellow, and faint green. I found them waiting after I reached the top of the winding staircase to enter through the little door—the one with the heart-shaped knob. As I crawled through the opening, the room seemed to enlarge before me, and it was filled with bright, white light. The seven looked up as if they were expecting me. Lovely faint music emanating from somewhere in the background served as white noise. I floated around them, and their genuine smiles welcomed me. Words were not necessary, but there was an understanding that seeped into my consciousness. Love was real and present here. Divine.*

*However, when I saw the women, I expected something else. For the women here were not my closest friends. They had each walked through my life at different points in time. There had been a few hurts, a few misunderstandings and lessons learned. These were relationships that were like a revolving door; in and out. They were not meant for a lifetime.*

*But what was this place? Where was I? Why was I here? How did I get here?*

*As I floated around the room, the overwhelming sense of peace and forgiveness permeated all the memories surrounding the seven. All I could feel was a deep awareness of them as lovely spiritual beings. I felt their love and acceptance. But more than their feelings towards me, I felt only love for each of them. It was overwhelming and beautiful.*

When I awoke from my dream, the euphoria present in my dream lingered. For the next two weeks, I felt energized by an inner light and centered spiritually. Love was the answer. Love was transformative. Love gave everything meaning. Love gave me peace.

> "Spiritualism is the understanding of the universe so that the world can be a better place."
>
> —FELA KUTI

*Chapter Five*

# Animal & Nature Spirit

# A Robin Marks the Spot

My friend's twenty-year-old son died in a tragic accident a year after his high school graduation. The loss of her son was devasting and unbearable. One day, shortly after his death, her husband gifted her a necklace with a heart-shaped locket that she wore around her neck from that day forward; inside the locket was a photograph of her son. She says that the image in the locket kept her son right where she needed him to be, next to her skin, against the beating of her heart.

One day she had gone golfing with her husband, but when they got home and were putting away their golf clubs, out of habit, she reached up to touch the locket. To her horror, her necklace was gone. She panicked! She asked herself, "When did it come off? How did I lose it?" Tears overwhelmed her. She wondered, "How will I ever find it?"

She immediately returned to the golf course and began walking over the course, starting at the last place she had been on the ninth hole and then looping back to the first hole and around the whole course again, trying to retrace all her steps. "Where, where, where on this large expanse of land could my necklace be?" she kept asking herself. She walked the course slowly, especially searching an area by bushes she remembered brushing up against and then the area beside a lake, but to no avail. She surveyed the ground near her feet as she continued walking. By the time she reached the eighth hole, she was empty-handed and frantic. Then she began to pray.

"Please, Lord, please help me find my locket. I just have to find it." She kept praying aloud and scanning the course in all directions. Then, suddenly, a bird—a Robin—flew across her path and landed on the ground in front of her. Her gaze turned to the bird. He pecked the ground and walked just in front of her, his head bobbing up and down. She says, "And then I saw a glint, a sparkle in the green right beside him. I stooped down to take a closer look, and to my relief and complete awe, there was my necklace. It was a miracle."

She said a prayer of deep gratitude.

Today the necklace remains secure with the photograph of her son inside the locket, against her skin, over her heart.

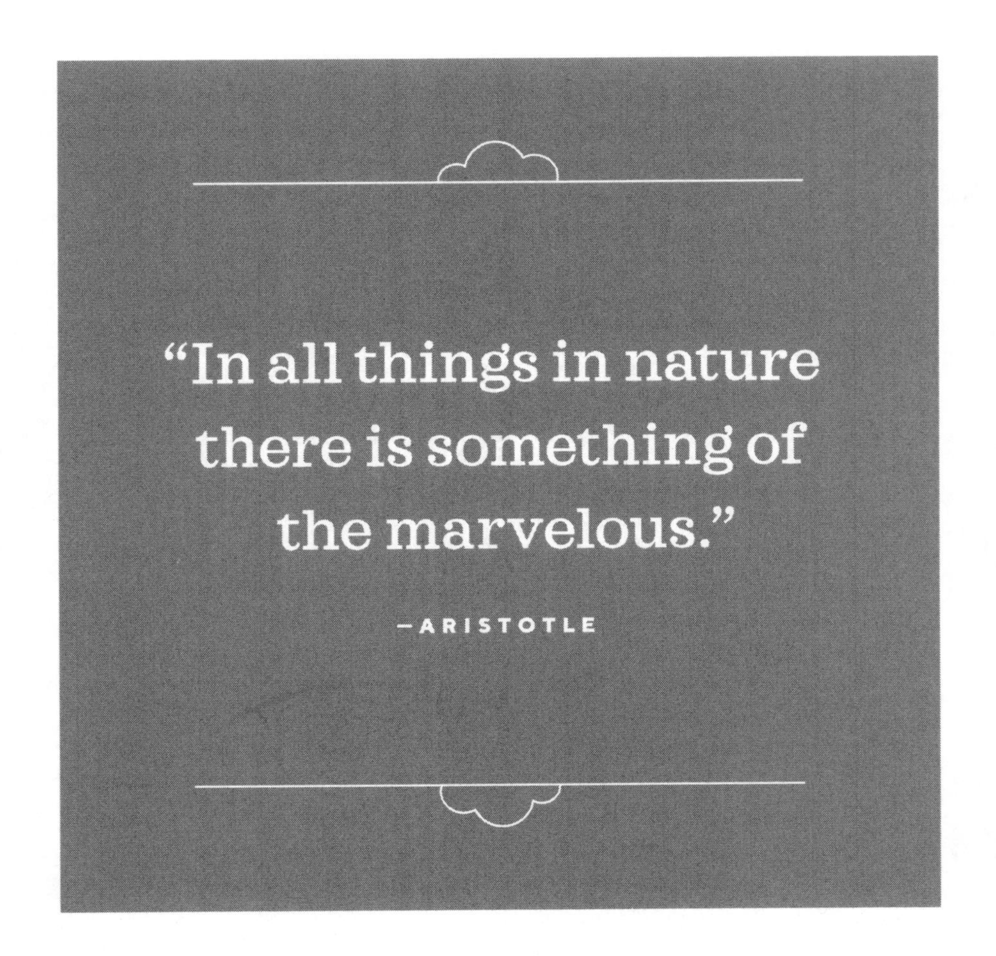

"In all things in nature
there is something of
the marvelous."
—ARISTOTLE

# Swimming With Glory

DEBBY CASON

For close to twenty years, I had a hankering for an up close and personal encounter with God.

From May 1994 through November of the same year, my husband, Roger Cason, and I sailed through the Fijian Islands, learning the culture and customs of the friendly native people. In May of the following year, after enjoying six months in New Zealand, we sailed back to our favorite Fijian cove, Vodovodonabolo Bay, off the southeastern coast of Vanua Levu. It was a quiet uninhabited cove where the natives from nearby Viani Bay came very occasionally to picnic or net fish. Through the clear turquoise water, I could see the white sandy bottom sixty feet below us when we dropped our anchor. We were so happy to have the cove once again all to ourselves.

As the anchor descended, I saw the coral-colored "beak" of a giant triggerfish ascending toward the surface, right near our forty-foot sailboat, *Dreamer.* I told my husband I knew this fish wanted to swim with me. He responded, "Well, not right now, Honey. We have a lot of work to do to tidy *Dreamer* after our passage and ready her for relaxation time. Maybe tomorrow."

During the ensuing nine months, I logged twenty-six swims with Glory. I named "my" fish Glory for the glory of God in all creation. Each swim filled my heart with indescribable joy. Not only that, but she frequently swam around our boat, just beneath the surface while I was exercising, meditating, eating, or playing my guitar and singing.

Without a doubt, I knew that God was answering my cry for a direct, personal experience. No giant triggerfish in the Fijian Islands would ever swim with a human being without being directed by God to do so because the Fijian men hunt them to feed their families. When we brought seventeen Fijian children to Vodovodonabolo Bay on board *Dreamer* to celebrate Fiji Day, we introduced them and their parents to Glory. They were flabbergasted at Glory's friendliness. Later, when the adults came back to the cove to net fish, our friends from Viani Bay specifically requested I "fish-sit" Glory so she would not get caught in their nets. That was one of the most memorable swims Glory, and I shared together, and Glory is now a legend among the natives of Viani Bay who looked on in amazement.

On the morning of our final departure from Vodovodonabolo Bay, I arose early to do my exercises and meditation on our foredeck. Glory swam to the surface as soon as I came on deck. She swam around and around *Dreamer* for two hours! Soon there was the sound of an engine entering the cove. It belonged to a Fijian friend who we would be transporting to Savusavu on our way out of the country. It was only then that my beloved friend descended to the coral head she called home. It was the last time I saw Glory. But she taught me, everlastingly, that God does respond to our deepest yearnings to know our Creator.

"Look deep into nature and then you will understand everything better."

—ALBERT EINSTEIN

# Off the Trail

DEBBY CASON

As was my weekly habit for the past two years, I pulled in front of the Arkansas Valley Humane Society and strolled inside to see which dog had been chosen to go for a hike with me and my sixty-five-pound Husky/German Shepherd mix, Cheyenne. The first part of the routine was to introduce the chosen dog to Cheyenne to make certain there was no bad chemistry between them.

Today, I put a terrier mix, Buster, into our SUV, and we drove towards Sleeping Indian to hike the Midland Trail with my friend, Betsy, and her dog, Amiga, who met us in the parking lot at the trailhead. No problems ensued between Amiga and Buster, so off we went. Five minutes down the trail, I shortened Buster's leash and knelt to have a heart-to-heart with him. I explained with words and hand motions that he was to continue following Cheyenne, a great trail dog who never galivanted off. When I called him, he was to come right here, pointing down at the ground in front of my feet. When I felt confident that he understood, I unclipped the leash from Buster's collar and rejoiced as the three dogs romped off down the trail in front of Betsy and me.

About fifteen minutes later, Cheyenne started barking wildly. Just to the side of the trail about twenty feet in front of Betsy and me, I see could see what was happening. Cheyenne was staring down a porcupine! I had recently witnessed the many porcupine quills that took a vet two hours to extract from my neighbor's dog. Contrary to my usual behavior, I started screaming

"A life of kindness is the primary meaning of life."

—LEO TOLSTOY

to Cheyenne at the top of my lungs, "Come here, Cheyenne! Come here right now!" Finally, she obeyed with no quills in her muzzle. WHEW!

A slight problem occurred because of my screaming, however: Buster was gone and nowhere to be found. I might insert here that the shelter did not allow dogs in their custodianship to be left off leashes when not on shelter property. I knew this but had faith in Cheyenne's and my joint ability to assure their safety, and I had never yet lost a dog. Besides, the animals were so refreshed and enlivened by these hikes that they were frequently adopted within days afterward.

Betsy and I looked for Buster for perhaps ten minutes, firmly calling his name, but to no avail. Betsy agreed to watch my pack and the two dogs so I could bushwhack off-trail to try to find him. As I traveled south, I looked everywhere and was saddened by the fact that if I lost this dog, the shelter would never again allow me to take dogs off their property.

Finally, I heard a Voice within me say, "Debby, if you want to find Buster, sit down on that rock over there, and let him come to you." No more than thirty seconds after I sat down on the designated rock, Buster appeared about ten yards in front of me. "Come here, Buster," I pleaded quietly. Slowly the dog walked toward me. When he reached me, I praised him, scratched behind his ears, massaged his neck, and then lifted his head up so that his eyes were gazing into mine. "Very good boy," I said, relieved. I picked up his leash, and together we headed back to the trail and resumed our hike. Two days later, Buster was adopted.

# Paisley

It has been said that people come into our lives for a reason or a season. The same is true of our pets.

In my final year of teaching, I experienced an unusual inflammatory illness. Some suggested it was stress-related due to a time of significant transition in my life. After all, I had been teaching elementary school for thirty-two years; this last year was a time of anticipating retirement, but also a time of letting go of a career I had loved.

The illness I experienced caused muscle pain, stiffness, and fatigue throughout my body. I didn't speak of it publicly, and only my family and a few close friends were aware of my condition. Eventually, it caused frozen shoulders. Prior to the illness, I enjoyed swimming in the local hot springs a few times a week. All I could do now was float on my back, gently moving my arms along the sides of my body.

Medical tests were inconclusive. I opted not to go on steroids, and I approached the inflammation with a plant-based diet, exercise, and therapies. Each week I had physical therapy for my shoulders, massage therapy for the pain in my connective tissue, a few sessions of acupuncture, and a variety of stretching programs introduced to me by my daughter.

At the end of the school year, on a whim, I visited the local Humane Society. It just so happened a litter of puppies had arrived that morning. They had been rescued from a place in New Mexico and had spent a few weeks in quarantine before arriving at the shelter. They were adorable black and white fur balls. One little one, who seemed extra rambunctious and alert, stole my heart. She seemed to choose me and crawled all over my lap, curling up in my arms. I signed the papers, took her home, and named her Paisley.

Responsibilities of a puppy were a Godsend. I took her for long walks to a local soccer field every morning, where we played and romped in the grass. Each day got easier; each day, I had a little bit less pain and stiffness. My attention and focus on Paisley gradually edged out the inflammation. Each day, Paisley grew larger into an unusual looking but beautiful dog. She had a small head in proportion to her extra-long body and a tail that grew longer and fanned out broader with each passing month. I adored her.

By the end of our first year together, I returned to my full range of motion and began exercising to the capacity I had been before the flare-up. I could run, dance, hike, and swim. I credit Paisley for helping me.

The day I came home and found her deceased from a horrific dog collar accident felt like a cruel trick. "This could not have happened." But it did, and while I was left with a deep feeling of loss, I also felt gratitude. Her life with me was meant for a season—my season of healing.

"Only the laws of the spirit remain always the same."

—NATIVE AMERICAN PROVERB

# Terry's Trips

Terry was our family's turtle. He was a cute, little painted box turtle.

During the winter months, he seemed caught between hibernation and awake, though we had all the right habitats set up for him. He was not eating, so the vet gave us some food to feed him using a syringe. He survived the winter in his glass aquarium.

In the early part of the summer, the kids were playing with him in the yard. I called them to come in for dinner, and while we were eating, my daughter suddenly cried out, "Oh, no! We left Terry outside!"

We all went outside to look for Terry, but there was no sign of him. We searched everywhere we could think but to no avail. Terry was lost. But we all held out hope all summer long and prayed that he would reappear.

A whole year went by until the following summer when one day the kids came running into the house, out of breath!

"We found Terry!" they yelled. "He was in the middle of the soccer field!"

The soccer field was nearly a half-mile from our house. How in the world? But upon close examination, we all agreed it was indeed Terry.

At summer's end, our family took an extended camping trip across the country. We took Terry with us, hoping to leave him in a more appropriate habitat better suited for him than the high mountain desert we lived in. We found a lovely place in Nebraska. He would have fresh water with brambles and meadows nearby. We were so grateful to find him again but even more grateful knowing he would be much more content living among his natural habitats.

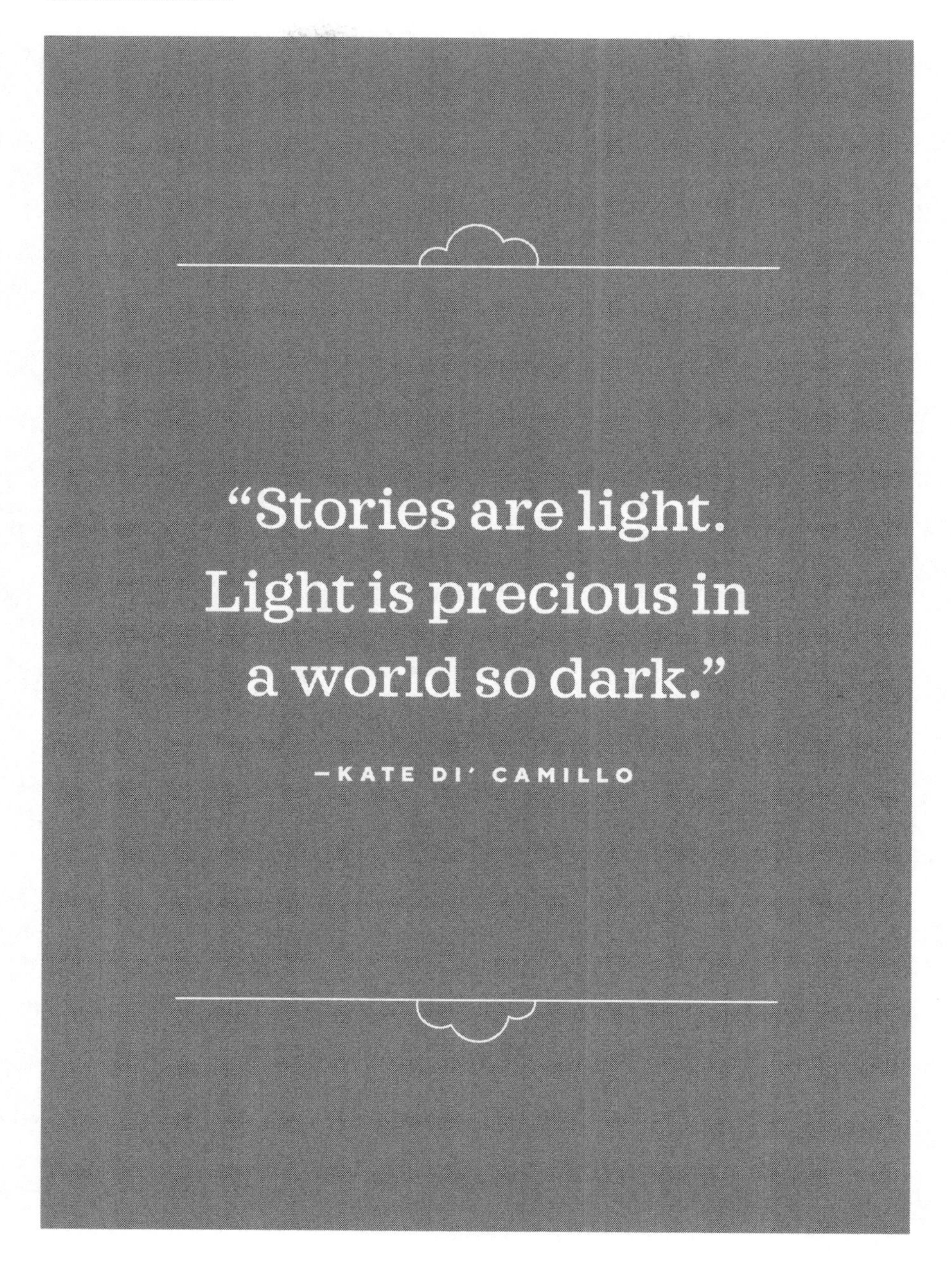
"Stories are light.
Light is precious in
a world so dark."
—KATE DI' CAMILLO

# My Spirit Tree

My tree stands tall and strong, on a hillside, overlooking the valley and picturesque Mt. Princeton, the signature mountain of our small town, rising in grandeur and beckoning to adventure seekers from the world around.

I first discovered my tree twenty-five years ago in search of an easy hike for kindergartners. It was about a ten-minute walk from where we parked the buses. We followed an easy dirt road and marched up a slope to where the tree stood. She was an easy tree to spot because she had a crook in her spine, which made her more beautiful. A magnificent Ponderosa with a rich vanilla scent, she was the perfect tree for our "Hug-a-Tree" activity.

The location of the tree and the beauty of the hillside view made a perfect Kindergarten Nature Day field trip. In small groups, the children explored, collected pinecones for birdfeeders, counted the rings on tree slabs, gathered autumn leaves for art activities, had an animal track scavenger hunt, used the five senses to explore the woodland, and enjoyed the freedom of the fresh air and beauty. Watching children in nature is remarkable; they are at home.

My family had a memorable family portrait taken from that hillside. Hikes in the area, picnics, and gathering in the view made for a simple afternoon of family time together.

I have taken many solo trips to my tree, where I sit against her trunk and write in my journal.

One year I had a "releasing" ceremony with a friend to let go of some heavy emotional weight.

This tree and location are little known to most people. I consider it a sacred space. I doubt many children or parents ever returned to the location after the field trip, for that experience was just a memorable and fun moment—so I prefer to let it live as one of the special days of a child's kindergarten year.

Usually when I visit my tree alone, I hug her. I tell her how beautiful she is and how I have loved watching her grow taller with each passing year. I feel her energy; I feel the love she bestows back to me. She has heard my thoughts, my joys, my sorrows. She knows my heart.

Recently the benefits of being in nature have been dubbed "Forest Bathing" by the Japanese. The research purports the benefits: relaxation, decrease in blood pressure, decrease in tension, increase in alertness and awareness. But beyond that, if we think about it as mutually beneficial, we may be able to tap into the spiritual benefits of communing with sacred spaces.

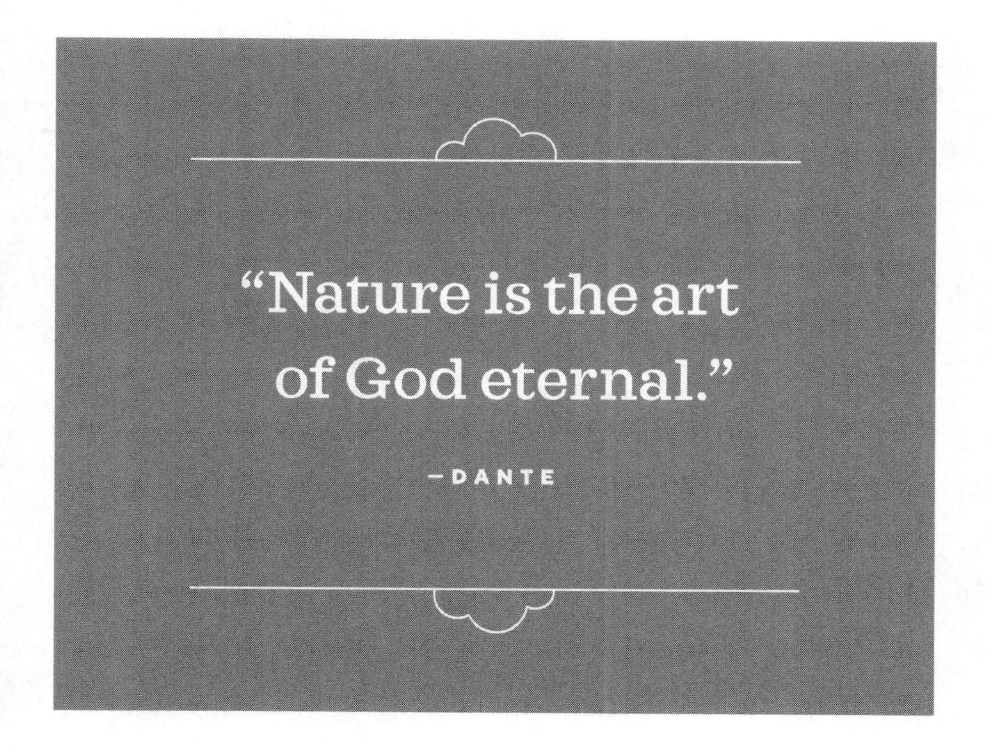

"Nature is the art
of God eternal."
—DANTE

*Chapter Six*

# Clairvoyance & Telepathy

# Confident in Knowing

JAN OHMSTEAD

By the time I was eight to ten years of age, I had noticed my knack for premonition dreams and precognitive thoughts. This ability guided me subtly and with little significance as a child. It was not until my high school and college years that I recognized my gift of foresight when peers remarked about my ability to foretell events and predict outcomes as they witnessed them materialize in the future.

The predictions of inconsequential events seemed trivial to me, but each occurrence illuminated my talent for intuitive and precognitive insights. I began to tune in and heed these premonitions if they were extraordinarily strong or predictive of significant events. These messages came in dreams or as thoughts that flashed through my mind while focused upon something totally unrelated. And I discovered an ability to sense the nature of people. My first impressions were spot on when meeting people for the first time. I could vicariously perceive the thoughts and feelings of others, especially when they were struggling emotionally. This type of extrasensory perception occurred even when merely making eye contact with strangers passing on the street.

Here's a simple example of precognition of an inconsequential event that occurred when I was somewhere between eight and ten years of age. While playing upstairs in my room one morning, out of range of smells, sounds, or sights from the kitchen below, an image of my mother's pear salad flashed through my head. I held that image for a second or two and continued with whatever I was doing at the time. About an hour later, my mother called me down for lunch. I walked downstairs and around to the kitchen. The table was set. Beside each dinner plate were individual salad plates bearing a leaf of iceberg lettuce nestling an upturned canned pear half, topped with a heaping tablespoon of cottage cheese and a dollop of mayonnaise. It was just like the image that flashed through my mind earlier that morning. Coincidence? That salad was neither a frequent lunch item nor a predictable pattern in my mother's lunch menus.

Here is an example that astounded my college housemates and solidified my trust in my precognitive abilities when I was twenty years of age. It was the beginning of a semester, a Sunday night. Monday was the first day of clinical practice for sophomore speech pathology majors at a major university. Each of us had registered for clinical practice, received a notice of acceptance from the department head, and been assigned a client for the semester. The clinical practice supervisor had provided minimal information about our assigned clients. We knew the name and age of the client, the parents' names if the client was a minor, and the presenting concern in need of speech and language intervention. Two of my housemates, also speech therapy majors starting their clinical practice, had spent the weekend frantically planning and fretting about their first day of therapy with their assigned clients. In contrast, I was calm as a cucumber and provided little information about my plans for the first day of clinic when they questioned my lackadaisical attitude.

By Sunday evening, both housemates were astonished by my lack of preparation for the first day of clinic in a department that threatened to kick us out of speech pathology and audiology if we didn't outperform our peers. It was a dog-eat-dog world in which the department head greeted us in the opening lecture of each semester with a recurrent threat that we should "look around the room because only half of you will be here by the end of this semester." The department culled our class of one hundred and sixty freshmen down to forty by the second semester of our junior year merely by GPA. It was an environment in which one could not show up unprepared for the first day of clinical practice. My housemates were distraught by my nonchalant demeanor and risky behavior.

"Let it be still,
and it will gradually
become clear."

—LAO TZU

Early Monday morning, we walked together to campus. They continued commenting on my reckless behavior. Why would I show up for clinic without a carefully crafted therapy plan? Why would I risk being thrown out of the department? My behavior was incredulous and stupid in their eyes, but I calmly reassured them everything would be fine. All weekend I had a strong premonition that my client, a three-year-old girl in need of articulation therapy, would not be there on Monday for her first clinic appointment with me. I shared this premonition with my housemates as we walked to campus. My client would not be there because her family was still on vacation. I had no way of knowing this, no way of receiving a communication from the family or the clinic, no way to verify my intuition with fact. And my housemates were horrified that I was risking my degree based upon some hair-brained psychic ability. I appeased them with a makeshift therapy plan in the back of my mind, but I was sure I would not need to implement it. If my client did show up, I could dash to the resource library and grab specific materials for an articulation screening and an informal diagnostic assessment. That would be an appropriate plan for the first therapy appointment. But I reiterated how certain I was that my client would not be there because her family was still on vacation. My housemates looked at each other in amazement and shook their heads at my crazy confidence in a premonition.

We entered the department building and walked up the stairs to the clinic. As we entered the reception area, I glanced at the large bulletin board for posting messages for student clinicians. There was a folded note with my name handwritten on the outside. I walked over and took it down, unfolded it and read it to my housemates, "Trisha will not be here today because her family is still on vacation." I showed them the printed message and they both looked at me like I was an alien or a witch. I just smiled at their stunned faces. They turned and walked over to the clinic receptionist to check in for their first day of clinic, for which they had anxiously prepared for days. And I had some extra time on my hands before class.

# A Shimmer in the Dark

Years ago, my eighth-grade son and I were walking along a gravely path one night on our way home from a basketball game. It was a short half-mile walk, but it was very cold, dark, and windy. He suddenly jerked around, looking over his shoulder and said, "Oh, my contact just blew out of my eye." Tyler's vision is extremely farsighted and requires a special and expensive torque lens, so this was serious.

However, without hesitation, I responded, "Don't worry. When we get home, I'll get a flashlight and come back for it."

"Mom, there is no way you are going to find my contact in the dirt, in the dark!"

Calmly, I replied, "Never say never. Just trust. Say a prayer."

Back on the path with flashlight in hand, I situated myself where I thought we were when the contact blew from his eye. I thought aloud, "And it's windy, so the wind may have carried it this direction to," as I made an arc with the light, pointing to the ground, "here." Boom! As soon as I saw a shimmer of light on the ground, I was on my hands and knees, carefully scooping the transparent contact from the tiny rocks, sand, and gravel into the cup of my hand.

I was neither shocked nor bewildered; I simply had a sense of, "I knew I would find it."

I walked back home and met Tyler at the door, saying, "Here it is."

Tyler, completely amazed, said, "Are you kidding?"

"Look, see? I have it right here! Just get your contact case and solution so we can rehydrate it."

Tyler wore his contacts the next day, none the worse for wear.

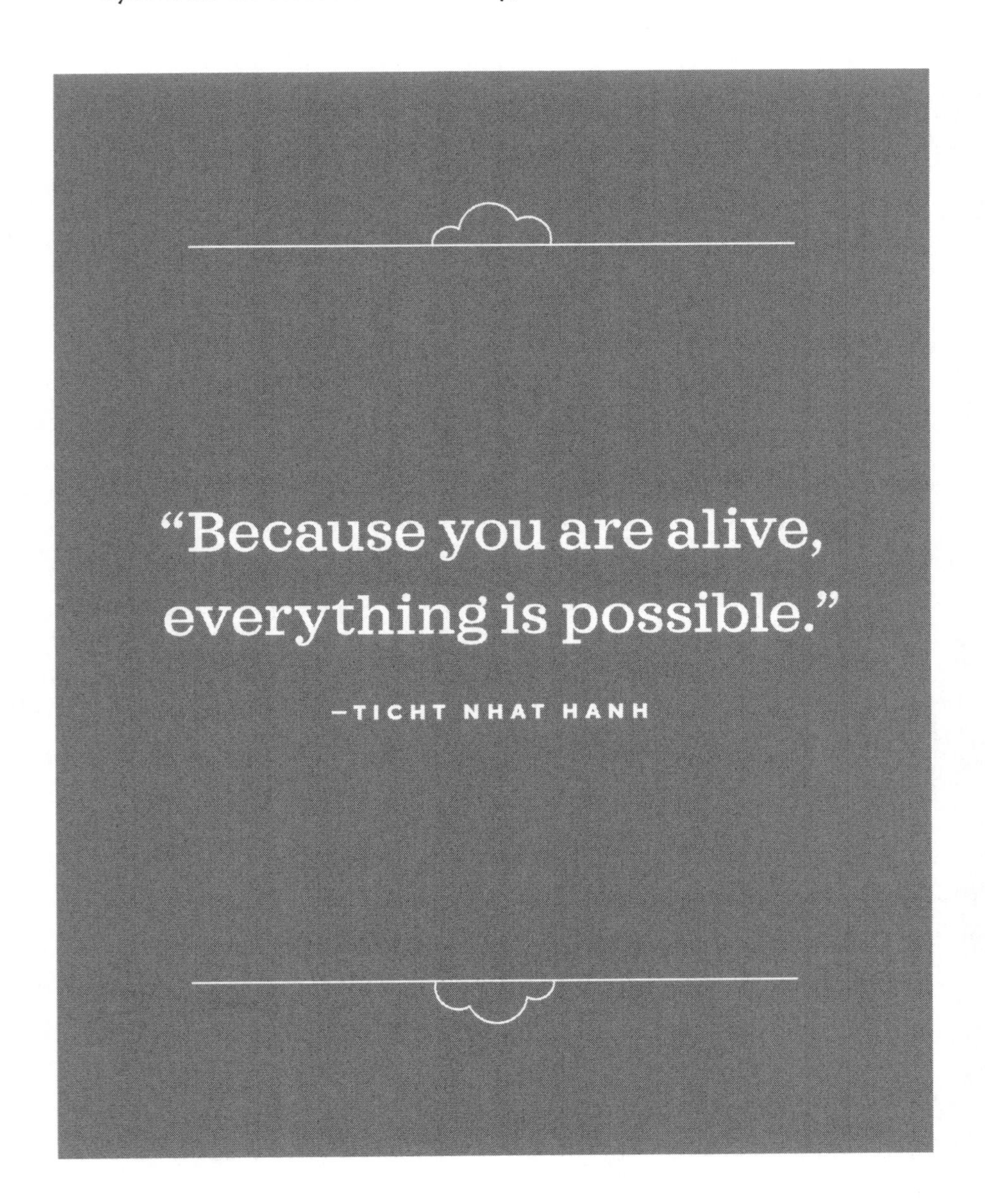

"Because you are alive, everything is possible."
—TICHT NHAT HANH

# Meaningful Experiences

CHRISTY SORDEN

- One afternoon after coming home from high school, I had a premonition of a blue and red car colliding with another vehicle on the Black Forest Road. An hour or so later, my dad came home and said there was a terrible car accident on the Black Forest Road.

- During my college internship, I was driving my Saturn coupe car on a busy highway. It was a very foggy day. I was sitting at the stoplight, waiting for the light to change. Once the light turned green, I heard a loud booming voice in my head telling me not to go. It was so loud that it startled me, so I waited for a moment at the light. A few seconds later, a semi-truck ran the red light through the intersection in front of me. If I had proceeded forwarded when the light changed, I could have died.

- After my grandfather "Papa" died, I had a dream. In my dream, my family went to visit him. We took the elevator up to the top floor of the hospital, and as the doors opened, there was a blinding white light—but it didn't hurt my eyes. The whole family was standing around Papa's bed. He looked fine. He appeared to be greeting each family member, but I couldn't hear what he was saying to them. But when he got to me, he said, "Christy, everything is going to be okay." I felt such a peaceful feeling.

- I have frequent dreams where I feel like I am visiting and talking to people who used to be close to me in previous years. It is like I am having a real conversation; I am asking how they are doing, and they are responding to me. It feels like Lucid Dreaming.

- For years, as I am walking or driving, when I get below or near a streetlight, for no apparent reason, the light goes off. This happens to me so often, and I can't figure out why. One day before my dad's heart surgery, I was out for a run and praying for him to be okay. I asked my guardian angels to show me a sign that he was going to be okay. Right then, the streetlight turned off. That familiar sense of peace overcame me. I was grateful just knowing they were with me, reassuring me that all was well.

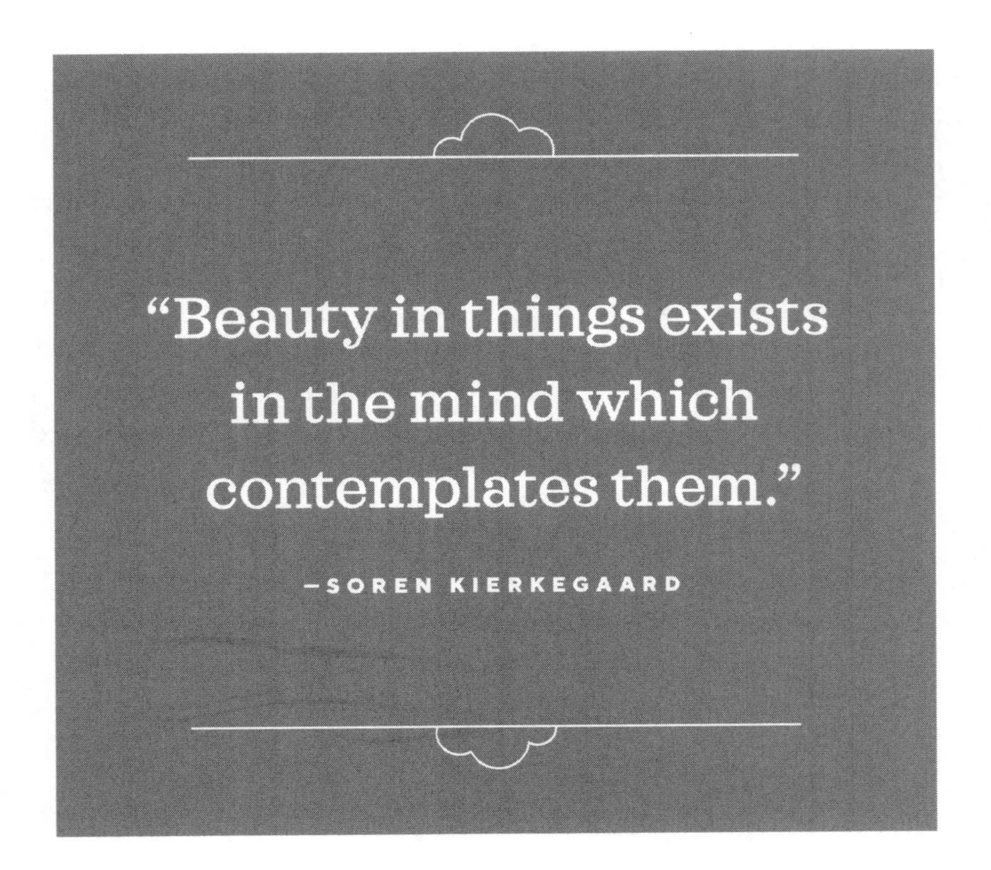

"Beauty in things exists
in the mind which
contemplates them."
—SOREN KIERKEGAARD

# Three Stories

**NANCY BEST**

- Once during a family dinner when I was a child, I heard my dad ask me to pass him the butter. When I did, he was surprised, which confused me. How could he not have asked me when I clearly heard him? Did his desire for the butter jump from his brain into mine? I don't know of any other explanation.

- In my late twenties, I was walking down the streets of New York City with a friend. The actor Richard Dreyfuss was approaching from the other direction. When he had passed us by, I heard my name called from behind, so I looked back over my shoulder, but no one was there except Mr. Dreyfuss. Even more strange was that he was also looking over his shoulder, though not at me, as if he had heard someone call *his* name. There was no one else around. What had we each heard?

- Several years later, I was telling a story to a friend that involved another person that my friend didn't know. As I was telling it, I was trying to decide if I should say the name of the person I was talking about. Before I even made the decision in my head, my friend said the name aloud. I asked my friend how he knew the name. He said, "You said it," but I know that I had not. This time it seems, my thought had jumped into someone else's brain.

"Life is really about an unfolding that is personal and enchanting—an unfolding that no science or philosophy or religion has yet fully clarified."

—JAMES REDFIELD

# Vivid Dreams and Predictions

AMBER WALKER

I was twenty years old when my vivid dreams began happening. My mom once confided she had experienced the same thing around that age. At first, the dreams were trivial and almost coincidental. I dreamed that my swimming coach was considering taking us to Hawaii for a training camp, and the next day it was announced that a Hawaii trip may happen. I dreamed that my mom ran into an old family friend at Walmart who was on her way to the hospital; this family had moved to California, and we hadn't heard from them for many years. The following day, my mom ran into this same long-lost neighbor at Walmart in Anchorage, Alaska, and she was six months pregnant on her way to a doctor's check-up.

Some of the dreams seemed to predict the future, while in others, catastrophes happened as I was dreaming them. One night while away at college in Utah, I had a dream that there was a huge earthquake in Alaska that damaged a specific part of the Glenn Highway. The following day, I learned that an earthquake had happened at the exact moment of waking up from my dream; Glenn Highway closed for repairs in the exact spot I saw in the dream.

One summer day, while I was taking an afternoon nap, I dreamed I was in an airplane near Denali, and the sun was bright. Suddenly the plane crashed into the side of a mountain, and when I opened my eyes, I could see the name "Kelly" written into my vision. I looked at the clock because I had an evening job and wanted to make sure I was not running late. Later, on the evening news, my parents learned that the small bush plane flown by a family friend named Kelly had crashed into a mountainside near Denali at the exact time (to the minute) that I woke up from the dream. Nobody survived. At that point, I began to get a little weirded out, and I became very closed off to my dreams and intuition.

It was not until nearly ten years later that I began to have the vivid dreams again. Since then, I have opened myself up more by reading about empaths and individuals who are spiritually gifted. As I have done this, I have had better dream recall and intuition, and I now understand how much this is a gift and skill set that should not be ignored.

Some of my recent dreams remain trivial, but in other cases, they have been profoundly helpful. Recently, I had a dream that a close friend was in trouble with alcohol, and when I reached out the next day, she confirmed that she had broken her sobriety. That same month, I also dreamed that my one-hundred-year-old great-aunt was in trouble; I later learned she had fallen and fractured several bones. I also dreamed that my grandmother was injured, and it turned out she had also taken a fall outside that day.

Often, even without dreaming, I just "know" that something is up. While in Peru, my boss was kidnapped at gunpoint and disappeared for several days. She traveled a lot for work, and since she worked from home and lived alone, nobody realized that anything had happened to her, but my intuition knew that something was wrong. Thankfully, she was able to escape and survived the incident.

At times, I also experience intense premonitions and have been drawn to thinking about people with whom I have little communication. In these cases, I always reach out and get a response that confirms that the person is struggling with something. Last year, I felt a strong urge to reach out to an old coworker, and he later confided to me he had been about to commit suicide when he received my texts and calls. I also feel very close to a family that I used to live with in Peru, and when they are on my mind, there is usually something serious happening.

I am so grateful that I am now more open to these experiences and am more in tune with my lucid dreams and claircognizant tendencies. I consider them a spiritual gift, and I look forward to continuing to learn more about how to harness these gifts to grow in spirituality and help others.

"They might not need me; but they might. I'll let my head be just in sight. A smile as small as mine might be precisely their necessity."

—EMILY DICKINSON

# Mom, Are You Singing?

The four of us were tucked in our sleeping bags, squished together for warmth in our tent. The kids were elementary school age and that morning just as each of us was beginning to stir, and blink our eyes open, I found my son looking up at me.

"Mom, are you thinking of the song, 'You are My Sunshine?'"

I was amazed. "As a matter of fact, I was," I said. "I was thinking of all three of my sunshines this morning."

The kids stretched and sat up, pulling off their hats and gloves, as their dad teasingly tossed pillows at them and scooted out of the tent to start the camper stove.

What amazed me about my son's question, was that I had been listening to the song in my head. In fact, I woke up to it. I was not humming it aloud, but for some reason I was hearing it in my mind. I sang that song to them often as we drove to school, but my son heard it, too, in his head, though we had been silent.

“Conscious experience is at once the most familiar thing in the world, and the most mysterious.”

—DAVID CHALMERS

# Is It Fate?

My husband and I met while on a weeklong student teacher exchange program in a small rural community. We had traveled with a team of teachers to experience teaching in a farming and ranching community with a population of one hundred. At the rural school, we were expected to observe each other while teaching lessons to students in the classroom setting.

The day I visited my husband's class as he taught a group of fifth-graders, I felt an immediate attraction to him. It wasn't just his good looks. There was something more tangible, like a magnetic pull, an almost familiar sense of knowing him, though we had never met prior to the trip. He later shared he felt the same when he observed me teaching my students.

When we returned to our college campus, the student teachers had only the weekend before we would be departing to various cities for our year-long teaching assignments. He had casually mentioned to me where he lived, which was only a short distance from my house. We said our goodbyes, but by that night, I could not sleep; I knew I had to establish some contact with him before leaving for my student-teaching destination sixty miles away.

The next morning, I woke up resolved to find him. My plan was to ride my bike to his apartment complex, but halfway there, I realized my bike tire was going flat. I dropped my bike off at a repair shop and walked to his complex, going directly to the manager's office. Timidly inquiring where I might find him, the manager told me the apartment number. It was then my heart began pounding.

Within minutes, I was tapping lightly on the apartment door. It occurred to me I had no idea what I would say to him. However, when he opened the door and saw me standing there, he took the worry from me by smiling and asking if I had eaten breakfast. When I said no, and explained about my flat tire being repaired, he said, "Let's go get your bike and ride downtown for breakfast." Years later, he told me as we were riding to the bike shop that day, with me leading the way, he heard the words in his head, "I'm going to marry that girl." He said he had no idea where that thought came from. But we spent the whole morning at the café, talking for hours. The next afternoon we hiked through the autumn leaves, agreeing to keep in touch over the next few months during our student teaching period.

By Thanksgiving, he had met my family, and by Christmas, we were having conversations about fate.

"Do you believe in fate?" he asked.

"Yes," I said, "there was just something about you from the first moment; I just had a strong feeling we would be together."

By that summer, we were engaged. Forty years later, we are still together.

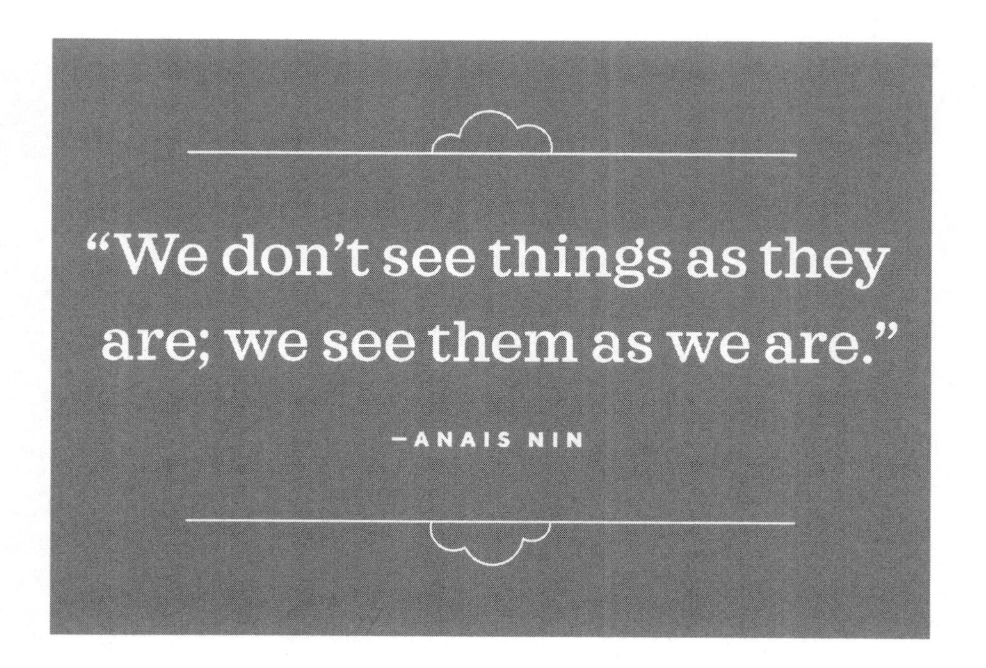

"We don't see things as they are; we see them as we are."
—ANAIS NIN

# Shared Dream

In 1996 I awoke from a horrific dream recalling bodies falling through the air. It was so disturbing and felt so real. I began to prepare breakfast when my twelve-year-old daughter entered the kitchen and said, "Mom, I had this awful dream. It was like a plane or something crashing, and people were falling through the sky." A short time later, my nine-year-old son entered, eerily reporting a similar dream.

A chill ran through my body. "How strange," I thought. We all had similar dreams." We spoke about the dreams briefly, but I did not want to alarm them, so we continued with our morning breakfast routine.

The next day I was at a café listening to music playing from a radio station. When a news report came on, I heard something about a plane exploding and stopped to listen for the details. I asked another patron of the café what had happened. "Last night, a TWA plane exploded off Long Island just twelve minutes after taking off from John F. Kennedy International Airport. They were headed to Paris, then Rome. Everyone was killed."

It was a devastating tragedy. I was shocked by the news, but also in remembering our similar dreams. A shiver ran through me.

How did this event find its way into our dreams?

"A single dream is more powerful than a thousand realities."

—J.R.R. TOLKIEN

# Can You Find the Backing?

My friend, Lindy, and I were attending our sons' cross-country meet. We were running in along the edges of the course, cheering them on, when Lindy suddenly said, "Oh! My earring! I lost it!"

Calmly, I asked, "Where were you when you last remember having it?"

"I'm sure it was at the start of the race."

"What does it look like?"

She showed me the one in her other ear, a tiny white pearl.

We walked back to the beginning of the course and stood alongside the gravely dirt road where the kids began the race.

"Around here?" I asked.

As Lindy confirmed we were standing in the right spot, I scanned the area. There it was—isolated in my vision among the many stones and gravel. I walked over to where I saw the tiny round pearl as if it were the only thing on the ground and picked it up.

I handed it to Lindy, and she smiled in awe, thanking me but then adding, "Can you find the backing to it now?"

“The world is made of mysteries and I was only a riddle among the millions.”

—MADELINE MILLER

# My Baby Brother

I was sixteen when my youngest sibling was born. In some ways, I took on a maternal role with him, those earliest nurturing instincts palpable with him. When I graduated from high school and moved from our Air Force base in Germany to the United States, I knew I would not see him or the rest of my family for another two years.

One day, when I had stopped to grab a bite to eat at a fast-food restaurant, I froze in my tracks, bag of food in my arms. I was overcome by a sinking feeling that something had happened to my little toddling brother. I became very worried. This was long before cell phones or email. I would have to wait for either a phone call or a letter.

Somewhat relieved that a phone call never came, I dismissed it as a longing to see my family. However, about two weeks later, I received a letter from my mother, which was somewhat unusual as she was not a prolific letter writer. Usually, correspondence would come from my father or perhaps news through my grandparents, who I visited frequently.

The letter stated my little brother had been hospitalized with pneumonia; that it had been serious, but he was recovering and back home. I immediately recalled the moment in the restaurant that had stopped me in my tracks. Relieved, yet somewhat mystified at the experience, I wrote to my mother, explaining how happy I was he was fine but how I had also sensed something was wrong. There was comfort in realizing the premonition had a happy ending.

"It is only with the heart
one can see rightly.
What is essential is
invisible to the eye."

—ANTOINE DE SAINT-EXUPERY

# Mia, Where Are You?

Mia, my sweet Australian Shepherd dog, loved to go trail running with me. One evening we set out for a run, a bit too late. We had run about three miles before the sun was already dipping below the horizon; the air was too chilly for the clothes I had worn. I was anxious to pick up the pace and get home when I realized Mia was out of sight.

"Mia! Mia!" I called, over and over—still no sign of her. I was in mountain lion territory, and dusk was not the time to be alone on the trails. I would have to go home and then return later to look for her, meanwhile hoping she might take another trail down and get home before I did.

When I got home and changed clothes, there was still no sign of Mia. I proceeded to make dinner. My family agreed she might show up at the door at any time, but as we were eating, I had a nagging feeling I should not wait. I scooted back from the table and said, "I need to go find her. I feel it; something is wrong. I have this sense she is not hurt, but something is wrong. I know she needs help."

I drove up to the overlook. The trail was below me, so I parked the car, got out, and called her name. I shivered from both the cold and the vulnerability of being alone on the dark trail. As I began descending the trail, the light from my flashlight scanned over the bushes and shrubs along the path. Then I saw it! A large bush caught my attention. I stared at its shape and what I saw was an image of Mia. It looked like she was lying down with her head

"The senses, being the way of the world, open the way to knowledge."

—MARIA MONTESSORI

up, looking at me. It confirmed what I knew. She was okay, but she needed my help.

I drove back home and gathered my family together, explaining the image I saw in the bush. "She needs our help; are you all coming?" They were skeptical, but agreed to join me.

The four of us parked at the lower trail and began our trek back up the hill, calling Mia's name as we hiked. Then, we heard her. She was barking! "Mia! Mia! We're coming! Keep barking!"

My husband and son were ahead of my daughter and me when I heard my husband say, "Well, well, Mia. How did you get down there?"

My daughter and I ran to catch up, and then we saw Mia. In an old, excavated mining area, Mia had tumbled down into a ten-foot-deep hole. It was quite wide but with steep sides. There was no way to get her out. My husband said he would go back home to get some ropes and a horse harness to pull her up. After my husband left, the kids and I talked to Mia, reassuring her we would get her out soon. Then, in that moment, she laid down into the dirt, settling into the exact position I saw in the image of the bush! She was not injured but needed our help.

Once we had the equipment in hand, my husband lowered the kids into the hole. They attached the harness and ropes to Mia, and we pulled them all up one, by one, out of the hole. It was a night to remember.

*Chapter Seven*

# Spirit Visitations & Supernatural Encounters

# Peruvian Ghosts

AMBER WALKER

As a child, I recall an incident where I saw visions in the clouds, including a crucifix that appeared supernatural. As a teenager, I had an encounter with a UFO while driving to an early-morning swimming practice. I downplayed these experiences after handling some embarrassing social ridicule from peers and family, and in all honesty, I harbored some doubt about my own grasp of reality. But when I began having interactions with ghosts in my late teenage years and twenties, I began to trust my intuition and believe in my supernatural experiences.

My first ghost experience to memory happened when I was home alone as a senior in high school. In college, I began having regular ghost experiences when living in an older building that was built on top of a swimming pool. It turns out that a little girl had drowned there, which I was not aware of until about six months into having regular spirit world interactions in the building.

But my most powerful and memorable ghost experiences occurred when I moved down to South America. I lived in Peru for one year in the house of my host family's grandmother, who had passed away a decade prior. A few weeks after I arrived, I began to have strange experiences at night. I'd hear someone sweeping right outside my door, but nobody was there. I'd hear the noise of chairs moving around the dining room floor at three and four o'clock in the morning. And sometimes, I would be jolted awake to freezing air inside my bedroom in the heat of summer (to the point where I could see my breath) and would feel the presence of someone in the room. On a few occasions, the ghost would sit down on the bed with me, and I could see a transparent human outline checking me out. This spiritual presence did not feel threatening, but rather it seemed curious as to why I was there.

When I finally had a good enough grasp on Spanish, I asked my host sisters, who shared the bedroom across from mine, if they had noticed any of these things. They laughed and told me that they were wondering if I would ever ask! To them, experiences with their *abuelita's* ghost were a normal occurrence. Peruvian culture is very open-minded to the idea of ghosts, and to them, it was never a matter of whether they existed; ghosts were simply an everyday part of life. When I had visitors and friends come and stay with us in the room next to mine, they always recounted tales of cold air and odd bedside experiences the next morning.

Because we were in a dangerous neighborhood, the house had six locking doors between the outside street and the bedrooms. The family only had one full set of all the keys, and my host sister Karely was the one in charge of them since she got up earliest for work. She would lock us into the back part of the house at night and then open all the doors in the morning. However, the doors locked automatically if you shut them, and one evening she realized that she'd accidentally left her keys in the living room and had locked all of us into the bedroom area of the house. Karely woke up at about 3 a.m. and panicked when she realized this. She whispered a plea for help to her *abuelita*, and a few minutes later, she heard a ton of noise coming from the living room. She crept over to the locked door and saw something shiny on the ground. Miraculously, her keys had been placed on our side of the door.

The following day, my host family placed a cup of Coca-Cola on the mantel by the picture of their grandmother as a thank you gift. That evening when we returned from work, some of the beverage was gone, and though I teased them about the concept of evaporation, I began to have a newfound respect for spirit world interactions.

Later that year, we took a bumpy bus ride to a remote town called Tembladera, a farming community where many of my host family's relatives lived. The town was famous for being built over an old battleground where,

The supernatural is the natural not yet understood."

—ELBERT HUBBARD

historically, Incan Peruvians clashed with Spaniards in the 1500s. We stayed on the floor of the home where their grandfather had lived and raised his family. Sadly, he'd had a farming accident and died in the very space where we were sleeping. The house had a sloping dirt floor and no furniture, running water, electricity, or bathroom space. At the back of the house, a large metal door was padlocked with several chains and locks. My host sister told me that the door used to lead to an outhouse but that nobody knew where the keys were.

We were there in the peak of summer, and it was unbearably hot and humid. We attempted to sleep sprawled out on the dirt floor, but it was too hot. After it got dark, as I lay on the ground chatting with two of my host sisters, the room suddenly turned ice cold. We heard footsteps pacing outside of our room, and then the door opened. A spiritual presence got down on the ground next to me and began breathing on my face in a loud, raspy, labored manner. I could tell it was a man. We all froze, slightly terrified. After a few minutes, the ghost got up and returned to the hallway, pacing.

For the rest of the night, he would come and lay next to me, breathing cold air on my face, and then return to the hallway to pace. At times, we heard loud scraping noises coming from the back door. After a few cycles of this, my youngest host sister freaked out and decided to sleep elsewhere. But Karely and I stuck it out because we had nowhere else to go, and I felt a strange sense of curiosity about it. This was the first time that I'd shared a ghost experience with someone else, and it was nice to know that I wasn't losing my mind. In hindsight, their grandfather's ghost was probably just confused as to why a strange *gringa* was sleeping on the floor of his home. The following morning, at daylight, we discovered that the heavy metal door at the back of the house was wide open, the padlocks open for the first time since the house became uninhabited.

The year after I left Peru, a new American volunteer stayed with the same host family and shared similar stories. She told me that one night, she decided to have a conversation in Spanish with the grandmother's ghost because she was tired of getting woken up all the time. Specifically, she said, "Abuelita, I'm here as a medical volunteer at the local clinic. I'm here to help. I love your family, and I will take care of them and watch over them. You don't need to clean the floors anymore." The sweeping and furniture rearranging ceased from then on; that was the last evening that she had a ghost encounter in the home!

# Passing By

**LAURA REIS**

My sister and her husband had arrived for a visit the night before.

Early the next morning, I was in the kitchen. Our kitchen has a doorway entry from the main hall of the house and is wide open towards the family room. The dishwasher is aligned with the back of the house so that as you open it, you pull the dishwasher door back in the direction of the doorway.

I was in the process of emptying the dishwasher and facing the family room. The doorway entry was to my right. As I began to empty the dishwasher, I caught a glimpse of what appeared to be a white flowing nightgown walking or maybe gliding past the doorway. Since the figure was near the guest room, I assumed it was my sister.

As I walked over to greet my sister, I softly called out her name, but no one was there. I looked down the hallway to the right, and I then looked left towards the guest room, but all was dark. I was certain I had seen someone, but whoever had been there was gone.

It left me feeling like I had experienced something rare, but I also felt sad that the encounter was so brief. To this day, the feeling I experienced from the sighting remains imprinted in my memory. I am certain that I saw a figure walk/glide by.

"It's not only for unanswered questions that we seek knowledge, but also for the examination of unquestioned answers."

—ANODEA JUDITH

# An Encounter On the Trail

**LAURA REIS**

One lovely autumn weekend, my husband, Mark, and I went camping with friends in the lovely Aspen Mountain, outside the Maroon Bells area. We were planning to camp for the night, several miles from the main parking lot. We were heading down a heavily treed Aspen grove, which was on a steep trail consisting of a lot of switchbacks. It twisted and turned in such a way that you could see the tops of the heads of those who were walking ahead of you going down, or if you were looking up backward, you would see the legs of those behind you on the next switchback.

My experience was odd because of this dynamic nature of the pathway.

Mark and the others were a bit ahead of me when I looked up, and standing there before me on the trail was a man. He was going up the trail as I was going down. He appeared to be about fifty years old, fair-skinned, bright white hair, light eyes, and he was dressed all in black. Not exactly how you would expect someone to be dressed, considering where we were on the trail. Nonetheless, I nodded and smiled as I passed him, but I did think there was something slightly odd about him.

As I walked along and turned down the next switchback, watching my step, I kept thinking of that man. When I looked up, there he was again! Right in front of me! He gave me a very strange, almost knowing smile but never said a word. I suspected he saw the surprise on my face as there was no way for him to get back down to the lower point in the trail without my seeing him!

I caught up to Mark and our friends and asked if they had seen or noticed a man on the trail dressed in the way I described, but no one had noticed or seen him.

The memory of him and his expression is very strong to this day. Who was this man? I was left with a feeling that he wanted me to see him and wonder about him.

To this day, I would love to ask someone to explain this to me. Or if I could see him again, I would ask, "Why did you want me to see you?" And "What is it that you hoped I would see in you?"

I am sure some people would think that I was simply mistaken. But I believe what I saw. I would like to know more about that encounter and why he wanted me to see him.

That is the feeling that still lingers.

"There are years that ask questions and years that answer."

—ZORA NEALE HURSTON

# United States Coast Guard Cutter Taney's Broken AC

SALLY INADA

Bang! Bang! Far off yelling. More banging and yelling.

I began to squirm off the middle rack of a Coast Guard crew bunk on the US Coast Guard Cutter Taney permanently berthed in Baltimore's harbor. I was sleeping aboard—or at least attempting to sleep aboard the craft—as a Cub Scout chaperone. My hips and elbows scraped against the thin sheet metal frame as the rack's quarter-inch plastic mat provided no cushion. I had not been able to fall asleep despite "lights out" happening several hours earlier. Everyone else in the cabin seemed to be deeply asleep, especially my husband, David, who was above me, and our Cub Scout son on the bottom rack.

But the banging and yelling outside the cabin was so loud and disruptive! How could anyone sleep through such clamor? As the banging and yelling continued, I could almost make out the words. Was something wrong with the air conditioning? The air below deck seemed stuffy and humid. I groped around in the dark for my shoes and a sweater. I had to investigate.

Imagine herding almost fifty Cub Scouts, from the youngest Lions to the oldest Webelos, into their racks, getting them ready to sleep. I wanted the scouts to keep sleeping, so I jammed my feet into my shoes and started creeping slowly toward the clamor. I had taken about three steps when I felt a little hand clutch at my sweater on one side and another little Lion grab for my sleeve on the other side.

"Please," Scout #1 asked, "Can you make it stop? It hurts my ears."

Scout #2 wanted to know, "Is something broken? Who is yelling? We're supposed to be quiet."

"I don't know," I said. "I'll go find out. You two need to go back to your bunks and try to sleep." I gestured for them to scoot back. But they did not budge. BANG! BANG! BANG! We all jumped at this much louder noise. It sounded as if several people were banging on a boiler.

"We can't sleep. We want to come with you," the scouts begged, clutching onto me.

"Alright, guys. Here, each of you take a hand. We've got to be quiet, though," I said.

"Why? They're sleeping through all the banging."

BOOOM! BANG! We jumped again. I could see a dim light ahead in the corridor outside our berthing area. That's where the sound was coming from. It didn't seem to get any louder as we walked toward the corridor. Though I strained to hear, I thought I could almost make out the words they were saying. It sounded like something had broken, and a bunch of loud men were trying to fix it.

We reached the corridor and stepped through the hatch. No noise now. The little guys let go of my hands as we stood listening. Still and quiet.

"I think it must be fixed," I said in relief. "Let's go back to our bunks and get some sleep." We turned around and stepped back into the dark area of the corridor, and began weaving our way through the bunks of the other sleeping boys.

CRASH! BANG-BANG! The three of us wheeled around again and retraced our steps. We could hear men yelling again, shouting for something.

"Can you understand their words?" I asked the scouts. Maybe their hearing was better than mine. We reached the hatch to the corridor, just where we had been before. We strained to listen to make sense of the voices. There was some humming around the dim fluorescent light, but otherwise it was a blanket of quiet again. We couldn't hear the snoring from our room now, either. It felt almost too quiet.

"Nope," the boys chimed. "Nothing."

"I guess we should get back to our cabin again," I said. "Cross your fingers it stays quiet. I need some sleep." The little guys reached for my hands on our second trip back to our bunks. We passed the same snoring scouts and a few restless sleepers.

Then, BANG! The loudest noise of the night crashed over us. And those yelling voices again! Now, what to do? I could see that the scouts were drooping, knuckling at their eyes, and starting to become a little more scared in place of their initial curiosity.

"Hey, guys," I said, trying to reassure them. "I have an idea. Let's see if we can play a trick on those noisy people. You two scoot back to your bunks, and I'll tiptoe back down the corridor and catch whoever it is making all that noise. Can you do that for me?" I asked over the noise. I was gently pulling them along, sidestepping back to our area. They were a bit reluctant, but I tucked one scout into bed and then the other. "Put your pillow over your head, so it's not so loud for you. I'll be back in a few minutes."

I headed out to the corridor in double time; I knew the dark, twisty way by heart now. I only had to follow the crashing, banging, and yelling sounds. But then, as before, all the noise stopped and it became eerily quiet as soon as I stepped over the hatch into dim light once again.

"Listen," I said behind the door, "I don't know what's going on in there, but if it's a game, you win. We heard you." I felt like I had to talk. There was a quality to the quiet as if something or someone was listening now. "I'm going back to our room now, and I won't come again. I just hope that whatever was broken is fixed now. Or please just leave it until morning. Good night and lights out!"

I stepped over the hatch and went back toward my bunk. I stopped to see if the little scouts were awake; no one moved. I had just made it to my bunk when I heard the soft echo of a bang, then faint faraway voices. I could still hear the clamor and clanging, but now it sounded as if it were coming from a great distance. I had to strain to hear it. Then, finally, all was peaceful quiet.

I gave up trying to sleep on the rack. I found a couch and dozed off until Reveille.

The next morning before breakfast and as we were packing, I told my husband and son about the late-night noisy adventure. I don't know if they would have believed me, but my two little Lions found me, one tugging his Assistant Scoutmaster Dad along with him. They chattered, gestured, and yelled out, "Boom-bang-crash!" while the dad looked at them and then me.

"This is a joke, right?" the Scoutmaster Dad said. "I've heard about scouting pranks."

"It's true!" the boys insisted. "It was so loud last night, and she heard it, too. Daaad, I'm not telling a story." The boys and I were trying to explain what happened, but we all ended up talking over one another.

"Let's get breakfast together, and we can sort this out," said my voice-of-reason husband.

Over microwaved scrambled eggs, paper cups of orange juice, and bagels, we told our story: The waking up to sounds of crashing, booming, and banging. Getting up. How the Lions found me. Walking down the corridor. How it would be super loud but then quiet down in the corridor—the same corridor on the other side of the bulkhead where we were sitting in the mess wardroom. We told of our two trips and of my last trip along. Scoutmaster Dad seemed skeptical at first, but after I verified the boys' stories, he agreed we should "investigate the hullaballoo."

I looked around the mess hall for the retired Boatswain's Mate, who headed the boat tours the day before. He had us climbing over the Taney as he lectured about the history of the cruiser: *She was launched in 1936 and is famed for being the last warship floating that had fought in the attack on Pearl Harbor. The Taney saw action throughout the Pacific during WWII and brought down several Kamikaze planes during escort duty. Later, the Taney showed the flag in the Pacific during the 1950s and 1960s, then transitioned into supporting the DEA on drug trafficking duty until she retired in 1986.*

We cornered the Boatswain's Mate in the quiet corner.

"What was the problem last night that had you banging around the boat for most of an hour?" I asked.

"Can't you fix the boat in the daytime?" asked Scoutmaster Dad's son.

"Yeah, it was so loud," said the littlest Lion.

"We didn't do anything last night," the Mate said. "I don't even sleep on the Cutter when there are guests aboard because sometimes chaperones use my cabin."

"We heard the noise. The two Scouts and I heard banging, crashing, and yelling for almost an hour," I repeated.

"And did you find out who was making that noise or what work was being done?" The Mate had a look on his face like he was trying not to smile.

"Was it a joke or a prank you play on Scouts? Because I don't think it's funny," I said a little too loud.

"Yeah, not funny," one Scout said.

"Hey, are you boys all packed out? The Scouts are policing their areas, so you better go join your packs. Go on!" the Mate said. My son and the two little Lions slowly walked away. When Scoutmaster Dad started to follow them, the Mate pulled him back beside my husband and me.

"What?" Scoutmaster Dad was startled. "I have to watch my Scouts police their area."

"Don't worry," the Mate said, "You'll have time. I didn't want the boys to hear this, but you're not the first to tell me about loud noises with yelling and banging at night. I've heard it myself when I've stayed overnight, too. It is very loud, like you describe. But when you try to follow the sound to the corridor, it goes away. When you back away, it gets loud again. It goes on for the better part of an hour, more or less. Sometimes more."

"Okay, so you've heard it. What is it? Fights on the pier?" Scoutmaster Dad asked. My husband began to hum the theme from the old Twilight Zone TV series. "Are you suggesting the boat is haunted?" Scoutmaster Dad asked.

"Well, to be honest, we did host that Ghost Hunter TV show last month. They got a lot of noise, the banging and such, on their tape, plus black shadows. They played the tape for me and I recognized the sound. Hard not to." He nodded to me, "Watch the show; you'll recognize the noise, too."

"So other people have heard it, and it's on TAPE!" I was stoked. "But what or who is it?" We were fully listening now. Scoutmaster Dad's eyes were big.

"I think what you heard is history," the Mate said. "I served aboard the Taney; the crew learned that one of the Kamikaze planes the Taney shot down came so close, big pieces of plane wreckage fell on board. That Kamikaze pilot was pulled from the water and treated in the mess wardroom/hospital area, but he died on the table. That is who I think walks the ship at night. We felt him keeping watch with us. The banging and yelling are from the plane wreckage and debris raining on the Cutter, crashing into her hull and deck. Damage control crew would have responded immediately, looking

“The ship is safest in its port; but that’s not what ships were built for.”

—PAULO COEHLO

for trapped or wounded sailors, maybe trying to shift some wreckage from her guns. So, what you heard, I believe, is a slice or piece of the past. Why some people hear it and others don't, I don't know. But you were not the first and will not be the last. Check out the Ghost Hunters TV show. You may recognize some of the audio. Now I've got more to do. Glad to have you aboard the Taney."

We watched the Mate move to answer other questions. Scoutmaster Dad rubbed his face. "Well, I'm not telling that to my son." He started to walk away.

"Wait," I asked. "Please, just a minute." I gathered my thoughts. "I agree; you don't want to dump this on your son. You might consider letting him be your guide in the discussion; see if he wants to talk. Don't lie to him. He did hear something extraordinary. He wasn't as scared as he was curious. I was a little kid who heard things, too. It was confusing and scary to be told I was imagining things or must have been dreaming. If he wants to talk about it, and he probably will, just listen to him. Maybe share some of what you heard as he grows up. Who knows, it might spark his interest in history."

Scoutmaster Dad stood quiet for a minute. Then he nodded and said he'd think on it, adding, "It was interesting meeting you."

David and I found our son, packed our gear off the Taney, and loaded up our van. I slept the whole drive home.

# Anybody Know What Time It Is?

SALLY INADA

When I was six years old, I got a blue Cinderella wristwatch for Christmas. I loved it. Back before cellphones, children received wristwatches to learn to tell time. The blue band looked so pretty on my left wrist. But I was surprised that the hands did not move. I would carefully wind the tiny knob on the side of the watch, and the hands would move, and it would tick—but within a few minutes, it stopped working. So, I stopped wearing it.

My mother gave me one of her old watches, also needing to be wound up using the tiny side knob. It was a real grown-up watch. But it didn't work for me, either. Later, I got my sister's hand-me-down Disney watch with Snow White on its face; but it also did not work. Then one day, I received one of my dad's old watches, big, clunky, and ugly, so I wouldn't wear it. Dad's watch sank to the bottom of my purse. If I could find it in the bottom of my bag and wind it up, it worked a little better for a while, but only if I left it in the bag and did not wear it. But even that was inconsistent.

When I was ten years old, my parents told me, "You need to wear a watch. You are growing up and need to be responsible." I was getting babysitting jobs and had a few afterschool-related activities. My new Seiko watch was water resistant with a seventeen-jewel automatic mechanism. My dad read the part about the seventeen jewels from the information in the watch box. I kept turning the watch over and over, looking for those jewels, but I only saw a linked metal wristband and a silver clock face. It was kind of disappointing when Dad said the jewels were inside making the watch work. Mom was certain that all my other watches had broken because I had not wound them up properly, or I had splashed them with water, or that I had lost or misplaced them. Or that perhaps I just did not like them. But this watch was brand-spanking new with a warranty, including all the latest bells and whistles. Maybe I needed twenty-one jewels. Mother put the watch on, and it worked fine. But when I put it on, it stopped working within an hour. Mother and I did this for a week, switching the watch from her to me. It baffled, confused, and angered my mother. She finally sat me down and said, "Never tell people you break watches."

My experience with watches became a moral failing, but it was something I could not control. I sure wasn't going to talk about it. In fact, I didn't talk about it for the next thirty years. Then came the day when my sister Susan and I were at a family gathering after my father's funeral.

Susan asked, "What time is it?"

Simultaneously my cousin Mike and I said, "Sorry, I don't wear a watch."

Mike's wife, Debbie, asked, "Are you one of the family members who can't wear a watch? Mike can't either. They don't work for him." Whoa! I couldn't believe what I was hearing!

"Yup, that's me. Never been able to wear a watch." Debbie and Mike told us it was in our family history; for some of us, "watches don't keep the time." They thought Susan and I had not heard about this phenomenon in our family heritage because we had grown up living overseas and were not able to attend many big family events. They proceeded to explain how we had family ancestors with gorgeous gold timepieces who could not use them. Wall clocks, mantle clocks, and case clocks all worked fine. But timepieces held close to or worn on the body did not work.

I have often wondered what genetic or biochemical element would cause modern watches or antique timepieces to not function. I have a case clock from the 1860s that needs to be cleaned and adjusted every few years. I once asked the repairmen in the shop if they had ever heard of something like watches not working on certain people. How surprised I was when the oldest repairman said it was common knowledge back in the 1930s and 1940s. He said his dad, the previous shop owner, told him that placing a copper penny to the back of the watch so that it touched the skin sometimes helped a watch to work. He thought it might have something to do with the body's electrical field.

"God is a subjective experience beyond the intellect. It is Pure Experience. Like electricity, it cannot be seen but it can be felt."

—AMMA

*Chapter Eight*

# Poetic Expressions On Spirituality

# As Time Goes By in Dreamland

**MARGERY DORFMEISTER**

Well, my poet friends are ailing and my hair is falling out.
As to the latter it's the cancer pills I have no doubt.
And I'm standing by the window and staring in the dark,
Looking for two light sticks across the river
From our House of Song.
I said to Leonard Cohen, "How lonely can I get?"
Cohen says, "Just hang on, widow woman,
You ain't seen nothin' yet,
There's music to be made
In this House of Song."
I was born this way. I had no choice.
I was born with the gift of a middlin' good voice,
And a big band leader, Larry Woodbury by name,
Tried to conscript me out of high school
To be the lady songstress for his band
In his multiple Houses of Song.
My parents were agreeable, could have used the money,
But you were in my life already, and you said, "Honey,
The grief those twelve male musicians would give you
On the bus, well, it wouldn't be that funny
Ridin' to and from those ballrooms of your Songs."

You can say I missed my calling to be the Doris Day
Of four Wisconsin counties by choosing my own way,
Stepping up my own songwriting and
Settling down to happiness with you
In our House of Song.
As Time Goes By, I see one light stick has gone out,
Where an angel and a cross mark your ashes strewn about,
Scattered by loved ones on the property you owned
At the foot of Sleeping Indian Mountain
Opposite our song-filled home.
The river's so low now I could tiptoe across to you
Without the crumbling bridge that's not in the purview
Of my House of Many Songs.
One night just lately, you came to me in a dream,
Crawled through a window, and your presence made ***us*** beam.
I say ***us*** because you know I never dream alone.
My dreams are always peopled with the souls we have known
In our House of Song.
"Meet Me Tonight In Dreamland," as the age-old song began.
Despite the distance between us now, you were the only man
I fully loved and trusted and would all over again
You are the solar battery fueling
My perpetual House of Song.

"Where there is love, there is life."

—MAHATMA GANDHI

# Inheritance—Solid as a Rock

MARIA WEBER

*for Marcy Adams (April 10, 1945 - August 21, 2020)*

My friend was a "rock person."
Our attraction to rocks was the first thing we discovered in common,
and it anchored our insight into one another.
As she was clearing out her house to move near her daughter in Missouri,
her final gift to me was a heavy, water-sculpted limestone rock.

I think back to times when my mother lost her friends.
What might I have inherited from her to prop me up today?
It would have been rocks, the timeless permanence of rocks.
Next to my computer lies a polished rectangle of black and white marble,
a gift from Joan to my mother Louise, her best friend.
I imagine their affection for one another
still vibrates within the molecules of this stone.

Both my parents collected rocks, starting with fossils in coal.
My mother labeled every find—with date and place discovered,
and its mineral type, if she knew it.
Special rocks found refuge in the six-foot bookcase
dedicated to their wellbeing in our spare bedroom.
Crystals made their homes on the windowsills
alongside Appalachian straw figurines.
Heavy specimens were used as bookends.

Today, my own rock pile resides at the foot of our west deck.
Particular beauties that I saved from my parents' collection
serve as palm-sized reminders of who they were.
The heavy limestone rock from somewhere east of the Mississippi
will forever marry memory to Marcy, recently metamorphosed.

My parents instilled my love for the igneous, sedimentary,
and metamorphic—real and metaphoric—
all you need to get along on this planet.

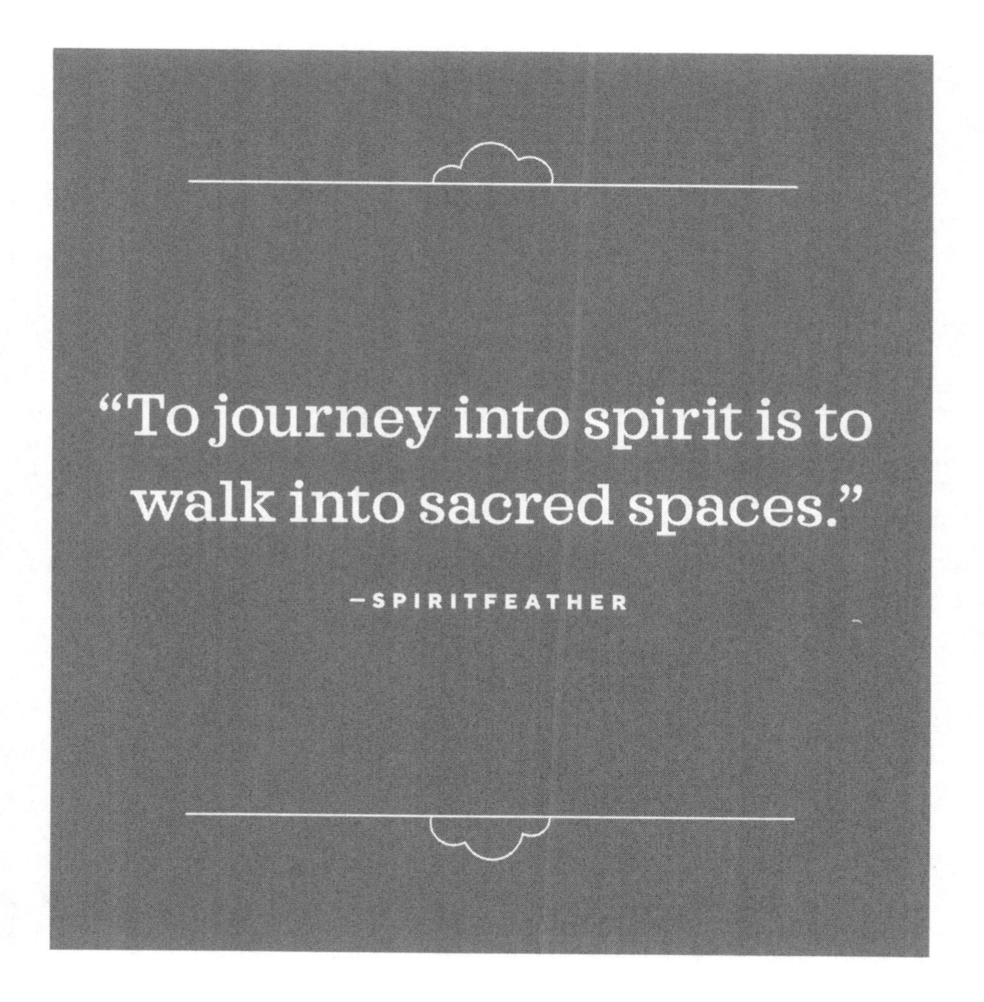

"To journey into spirit is to walk into sacred spaces."
—SPIRITFEATHER

# A Brief Visit

Dad floated through the room
In a wispy white blur.
His feet were not visible
In the cloudy velour,
But his cheeks were ruddy red,
His eyes sparkly blue,
His spirit was at peace,
This much I knew.
Four months now marked
The day he passed.
I called out to him calmly;
I was not aghast.
"Wait! Dad, wait!" I implored.
This was my Dad, whom I adored,
But his response was simply
A dimple in his chin.
Between here and there, the space was thin.
How he smiled! How he glowed!
Radiance and light
I knew in this moment,
He was bathed in Love's delight.

Then he was gone
As fast as he had come.
There were no hums or harps or heavenly songs,
But Dad was at peace, and happy as could be,
This was his message
When he came to visit me.

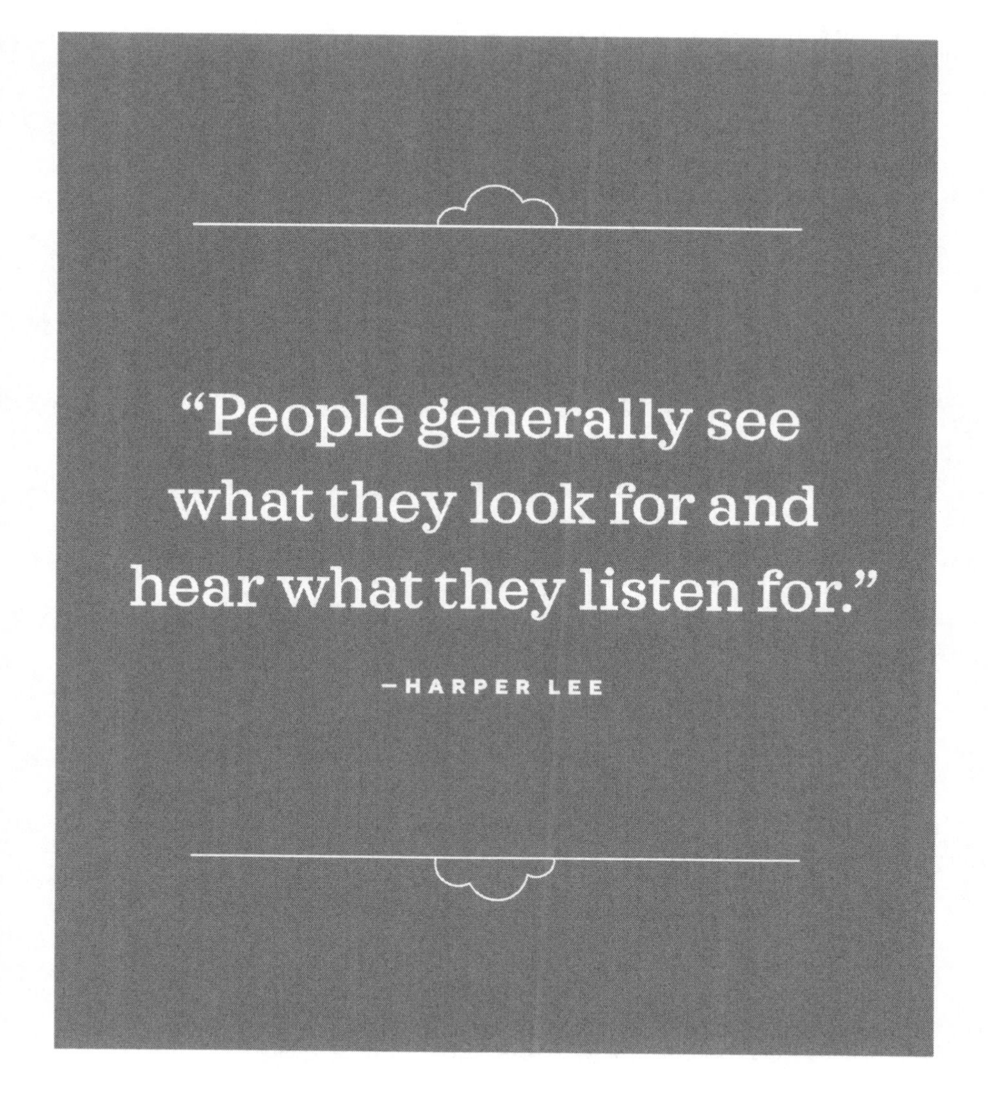

"People generally see what they look for and hear what they listen for."
—HARPER LEE

# The Circle

**GROVER ELLWOOD**

Our lives are a circle
No real beginning or end
We live in spirit before this life
And again,
When the journey is done.

Those that come into our lives
During this brief time on earth
Share in our travel,
And some help us carry the load.

There are but a few
Who carry us for a while.
Those that carry us
As we carry them,
Will be with us forever.

In the never-ending circle.

Find peace and comfort in this circle
Knowing that the love
That radiates from its light
Is carrying you now.

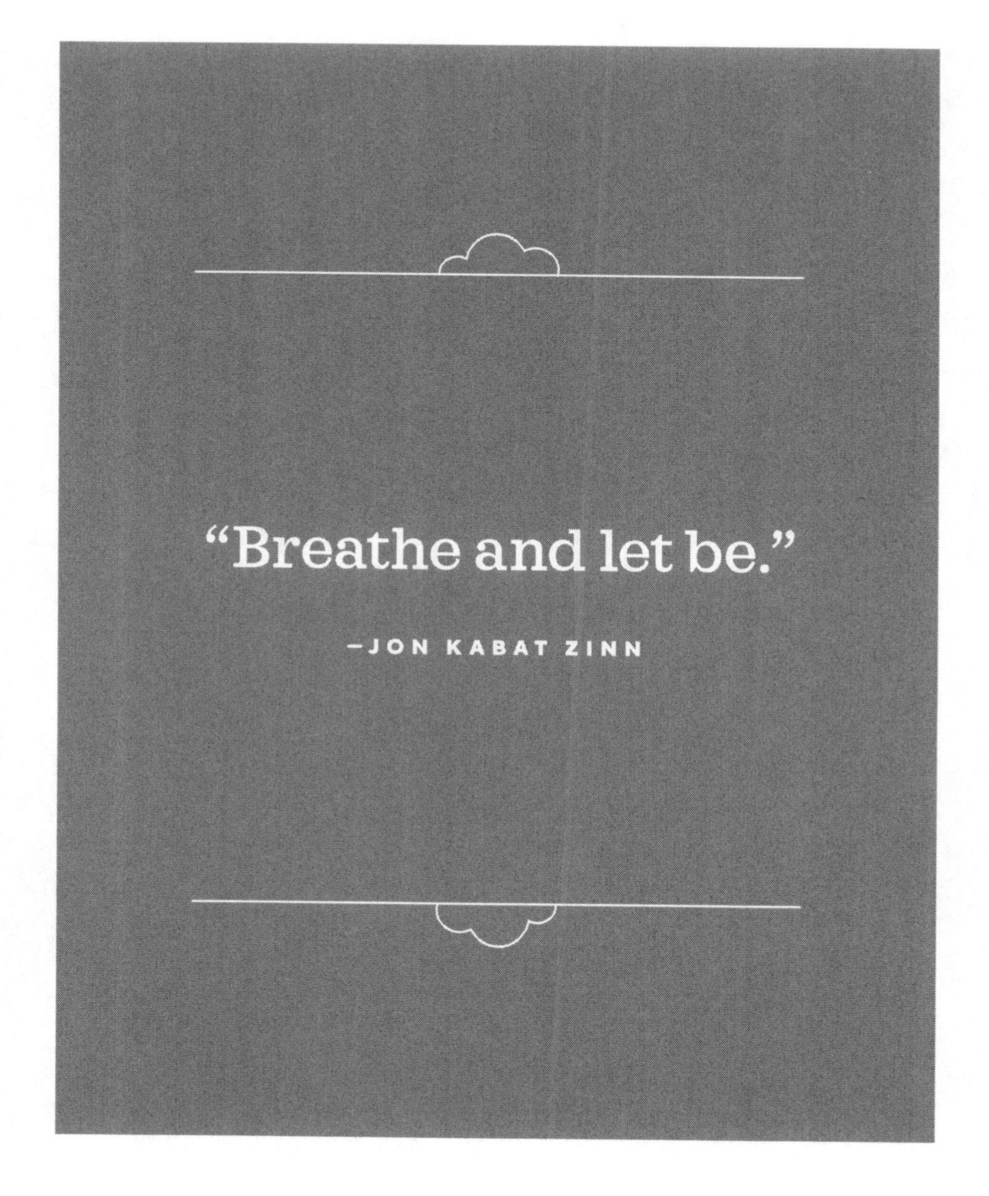
"Breathe and let be."
—JON KABAT ZINN

# Transcen-Dance

## ROSIE FEDORA

Prologue
*The clay dreams of becoming*
*From the source of everything*
    *A vessel imagined.*
*The clay dreams of turning*
*From hand to hand*
    *A vessel formed.*
*The clay dreams of dancing*
*From the fire*
    *A vessel born.*

The shawl draped her body as she lay quietly unaware,
Of the tassels that danced like whispers in the air.
Like whispers they danced along the contours of her shape,
As if her body was a hidden landscape.

With bowls and baskets in the long shadows of the sun,
She stood reminded of a life she had once begun.
Collecting embers from the night,
Ensured the journey and the next fire's light.
With every step forward, she never turned around,

Leaving traces of embers along the dry ground.

Still the shawl draped her body like a second skin,
Now grown faded and thin.
Still the tassels danced like memories often do
A whisper, "I'm ready to dance with you."
To which the woman replied,
"The woman who danced across the sky was not I.
My feet are too thick and slow
Like tree roots, they grow."

Shawl whispered once more,
"You have danced with me before."
Softly the woman spoke, "I don't recall."
"You will remember," said Shawl.

"Twirl me, twirl me around," Shawl said. "What do you see?"
Looking down, she spun around with her feet.
Spinning faster and faster, until she pushed off with her toe,
Holding onto the embers, she tended long ago
The bowl spilled out across the sky, far below.

Shawl pointed, "See the many colors of your past.
Your life's journey left a path."
Tears fell sweetly as her vision cleared.
For the first time, she saw beyond her fears.

"The light you saw in the eyes of others
You cared for like sisters and brothers,
The fire's embers burn . . . for you."
The woman could see this was true.

The sky darkened, and the woman felt afraid.
She wrapped herself in the shawl, covering her face.

Overcome with fear, she gasped,
Tightly holding Shawl in her grasp.
Shawl pleaded, "Open your arms and catch the wind."
The woman called back, "Tell me my story again."

The stars sang out, "Reach for us, try to be bold."
But she answered, "My hands are too stiff and old."
The fabric billowed as she tumbled far
Until Shawl caught the tip of a star.

As the woman dangled in the dark, she could see the light,
The colors were so vivid and bright.
She felt ready to let go
Of the pain, she held from far below.

She moved with ease across the sky,
Seeing beyond the horizon, in her mind's eye.
And her feet were dancing.

Still, Shawl draped her body like a second skin,
Shining with the colors therein.
Still, the tassels danced along the contours of her shape,
Joyfully resounding across the skyscape:
"Come dance! Come dance!
The day is new!"

**Authors Note:**

This narrative poem is dedicated to Donna and Delores, two inspiring women who have met life's challenges with soulfulness and grace.

Written intentionally for interpretive dance, the narrative hints at grace and our connection to something deeper that exists inside all of us, the Divine spark.

"I am in you and you in me, mutual in Divine Love."

—WILLIAM BLAKE

# CONCLUSION

*"To see a world in a grain of sand*
*And heaven in a wildflower*
*Hold infinity in the palm of your hand*
*And eternity in an hour."*
*—William Blake.*

*"You are Divine Love*
*Connected at all times to Source*
*Divine Love is when you see God in*
*Everyone and everything you encounter."*
*—Wayne Dyer.*

Thank you for sharing
in these experiences.
May your own magical, mystical, marvelous moments
bring profound meaning for you.

**Kathleene Keidel**
**February 2021**

# GLOSSARY OF TERMS

***After Death Experience***
An experience one may have with a deceased love one; may be a visual or auditory visitation or hallucination. This may include a symbolic message or a sign that a deceased loved one is nearby. Often the message received is that ***all is well***.

***Angel Guardian***
People often have experiences that may be perceived as "being led to an answer" or "being saved from harm," and the angel guardian is credited to being in the right place at the right time.

***Animal Spirit***
People often receive messages from an animal. It may come from a pet or animal in nature that appears at a time the person is in crisis or in need. Some believe in their animal tokens as a source of strength and healing.

***Astral Projection***
This occurs when a person feels their soul leaving their body and travel beyond their physical reality. This may occur in a deliberate exercise, or it may occur in a dream state. Often a person believes they have encountered heaven and can describe it with vivid sensory detail. Some people believe

they can connect with other souls in the dream state. This is a temporary experience, and the soul returns to its body.

***Auditory Hallucination***
A person may hear the voice of a loved one who is not in the room. They may hear the voice of a deceased loved one. They may hear unexplained ethereal music, singing, or other sounds.

***Automatic Drawing***
This occurs when a person allows their hand to freely draw without any thought of a subject. They place their hand on the paper and allow their hand and arm to flow without any concept of time. It is a process of allowing the soul to draw without any interference from the person. Often a form takes shape that has meaning or metaphor to the person drawing.

***Automatic Writing***
This is like automatic drawing. The person allows thoughts to pour out in writing form without any interference or internal critical voice. The writer writes as fast as possible, like pouring water from a vessel. Thoughts and patterns may emerge on the paper that hold significance to the writer.

***Clairalience***
The sense of smell triggers a memory, or a memory triggers a sense of smell.

***Clairaudience***
The sense of hearing triggers a memory, or a memory triggers the sense of hearing.

***Claircognizance***
A person has a clear understanding of events by "just knowing."

***Clairsentience***
A person can receive information through a strong sense of feeling or energy fields.

***Clairvoyance***

A person can perceive future events before they happen.

***Divine Intervention***

The belief that God or an angel has intervened for the good.

***Dreams***

Dreams are considered windows to the soul; the unconscious mind can help a person make sense of events by understanding the symbolism in dreams.

***Lucid Dreaming***

This is when one is aware that they are dreaming. The dreamer can sometimes control the events in the dream. It is sometimes defined as awareness of your awareness even though you are dreaming.

***Nature Spirit***

Often people find messages and strength in nature. This may be found in plants, rocks, animals, or the beauty of a landscape.

***Near Death Experience***

When a person is declared physically dead, yet has an experience usually related to observing their body or traveling to heaven, but then survives to relay their profound experience.

***Precognition***

Like clairvoyance, it is the ability to see events before they occur.

***Premonition***

This is a strong feeling regarding something that is about to happen. Often a premonition relates to a feeling that something bad is about to occur.

***Serendipity***

This is sometimes considered "a stroke of luck" when happy events occur in an unexpected way.

***Synchronicity***
Events that are unrelated but come together in a good way; often considered coincidences by some but considered meaningful happenstance by others.

***Spirit Visitation***
The belief that deceased loved ones or individuals make their "presence" known. It may happen while awake, while asleep, in a new place, or in a time of life changes. Often the spirit visits to deliver a message or to "check-in." This can happen while wide awake or in a lucid dreaming state. Some people believe they have brief encounters with spirits yet without receiving a message or understanding of the visit.

***Telepathy***
This is known as "reading one's mind." Some people believe they can communicate with others without the usual method of speaking and listening.

***Visual Hallucination***
When a person sees something that others don't see. Some people believe they have had conversations or experiences with someone who felt real at the moment. When they try to piece the facts together, they believe what they encountered was an experience with an angel or spirit.

# QUOTES

Amma. Born 1953. (Indian Hindu spiritual leader, guru, and humanitarian.)
*"The real purpose of life is to experience the divinity within."*
*"God is a subjective experience beyond the intellect. It is Pure Experience. Like electricity, it cannot be seen but It can be felt."*

Anaya, Rudolfo. 1937-2020. (American author, one of the founders of Chicano literature.)
*"The tragic consequences of life can be overcome by the magical strength that resides in the human heart."*

Andreas, Brian. Born 1956. (American writer and artist.)
*"She said she cried at least once a day. Not because she was sad, but because the world was so beautiful, and life was so short."*

Angelou, Maya. 1928-2014. (American poet.)
*"Life is not measured in the breaths we take, but in the moments that take our breath away."*
*"Spirit is an invisible force made visible in all life*

Aristotle. 384 BC-322 BC. (Greek philosopher.)
*"In all things of nature there is something of the marvelous."*

Bennett, Roy T. (American author.)
*"When one has a grateful heart, life is so beautiful."*

Blake, William. 1757-1827. (English poet.)
*"To see a world in a grain of sand, heaven in a wildflower, hold infinity in the palm of your hand and eternity in an hour."*
*"I am in you and you are in me, mutual in Divine Love."*

Chalmers, David. "Born 1966. (Australian philosopher and cognitive scientist.)
*"Conscious experience is at once the most familiar thing in the world and the most mysterious."*

Chopra, Deepak. Born 1946. (Indian American author and alternative medicine advocate.)
*"Religion is belief in someone else's experience; Spirituality is having your own experience."*

Coehlo, Paulo. Born 1947. (Brazilian lyricist and novelist.)
*"Sometimes you have to travel a long way to find what is near."*
*"The ship is safest when it's in its port; but that's not what ships were built for."*
*"A brush with death always helps us to live our lives better."*

Cummings, E.E. 1894-1962. (American Poet.)
*"I carry your heart. I carry it in my heart."*

Dante. 1265-1321. (Italian poet.)
*"Nature is the art of God eternal."*

Dass, Ram. 1931-2019. (American author, psychologist, and spiritual teacher.)
*"Be still. The quieter you become, the more you hear."*

De Chardin, Pierre Teilhard 1881-1955. (French philosopher.)
*"We are not human beings having a spiritual experience. We are spiritual beings having a human experience."*

De Saint-Exupery, Antoine. 1900-1944. (French writer, author of *The Little Prince*.)
*"It is only with the heart one can see rightly. What is essential is invisible to the eye."*

Di'Camillo, Kate. Born 1964. (American author of *The Tale of Despereaux*.)
*"Stories are Light. Light is precious in a world so dark."*

Dickinson, Emily. 1830-1886. (American poet.)
*"They might not need me; but they might. I'll let my head be just in sight. A smile as small as mine, might be precisely their necessity."*

Dyer, Wayne. 1940-2015. (American self-help and spiritual author.)
*"You are Divine Love, connected at all times to Source. Divine Love is when you see God in everyone and everything you encounter."*

Einstein, Albert. 1879-1955. (German scientist.)
*"Look deep into nature and then you will understand everything better."*
*"There are two ways to live your life. If nothing is a miracle and if everything is a miracle."*
*"The only source of knowledge is experience"*
*"The more I study science the more I believe in God."*

Gandhi, Mahatma. 1869- 1948. (Indian lawyer, anti-colonial nationalist, and political ethicist.)
*"Where there is love, there is life."*
*"Take care of this moment."*

Hanh, Thich Nhat. Born 1926. (Vietnames Buddhist monk, peace activist.)
*"Because you are alive, everything is possible."*

Hume, David. 1711-1776. (Scottish philosopher.)
*"Beauty in things exists in the mind which contemplates them."*

Hurston, Zora Neale. 1891-1960. (American author.)
*"There are years that ask questions and years that answer."*

Judith, Anodea. Born 1952. (American author, therapist, body-mind integration.)
*"It's not only for unanswered questions that we seek knowledge, but also for the examination of unquestioned answers."*

Jung, Carl. 1875-1961. (Swiss psychiatrist and psychoanalyst.)
*"Who looks outward dreams, who looks inward awakens."*

Hubbard, Elbert. 1856-1915. (American writer, artist, and philosopher.)
*"The supernatural is the natural not understood."*

Keats, John. 1795-1821. (English Romantic poet.)
*"Nothing becomes real until you experience it."*

Kierkegaard, Soren. 1813-1955. (Danish philosopher.)
*"The thing is to understand myself: the thing is to find a truth which is true for me, to find the idea for which I can live and die. That is what I now recognize as the most important thing."*
*"Life can only be understood backwards, but it must be lived forward."*

Kipling, Rudyard. 1865-1936. (English journalist, short story writer, poet, and novelist.)
*"This is a brief life, but in its brevity, it offers us some splendid moments, some meaningful adventures."*

Kuti, Fela. 1938-1997. (Nigerian multi-instrumentalist, bandleader, composer, political activist.)
*"Spiritualism is the understanding of the universe so that the world can be a better place."*

Lee, Harper. 1926-2016. (American author.)
*"People generally see what they look for and hear what they listen for."*

L'Engle, Madeline. 1918-2007. (American writer.)
*"For the things that are seen are temporal, but things that are unseen are eternal."*

Micah 6:8 (The Holy Bible)
*"Seek justice, love kindness, and walk humbly with God."*

Miller, Madeline. Born 1978. (American author.)
*"The world was made of mysteries and I was only a riddle among the millions."*

Montessori, Maria. 1870-1952. (Italian physician and educator.)
*"The senses, being the way of the world, open the way to knowledge."*

Morrison, Toni. 1931-2019. (American author.)
*"Love is or it ain't. Thin love ain't love at all."*

Myss, Carolyn. Born 1952. (American author.)
*"When you approach intuitive methods with respect, you become open to hearing from your interior channels."*

Native American Proverb
*"Only the laws of the spirit remain always the same."*

Nin, Anais. 1903-1977. (French Cuban American writer.)
*"We don't see things as they are, we see them as we are."*

Nouwen, J.M. 1932-1996. (Dutch Catholic priest, theologian, and writer.)
*"The spiritual life does not remove us from the world but leads us deeper into it.*

Overmire, Lawrence. Born 1957. (American poet.)
*"Listen to the silence to hear the heartbeat of the universe."*

Redfield, James. Born 1950. (American author, writing widely on human spiritual awareness.)
*"Life is really about an unfolding that is personal and enchanting—an unfolding that no science or philosophy or religion has yet fully clarified."*

Rohr, Richard. Born 1943. (American author, spiritual writer.)
*"God comes to us disguised as our life."*

Rumi. 1207-1273. (Persian poet.)
*"Be watchful. The grace of God appears suddenly. It comes without warning to an open heart." "Love is the bridge between you and everything."*
*"A pure heart open to the light will be filled with the very essence of truth."*

Sledge, Rev. Sharlande. Born 1952. (Contemporary American poet and pastor.)
*"Thin places," the Celts call this space, both seen and unseen, where the door between the world and the next is cracked open for a moment and the light is not all on the other side. God shaped space. Holy."*

Spiritfeather
*"To journey into spirit is to walk into sacred spaces."*

Swedenborg, Emanuel. 1688-1772. (Swedish theologian, scientist, philosopher, and mystic.)
*"A life of kindness is the primary meaning of divine worship."*

Taplin, Beau. Born 1988. (Australian poet.)
*"Sometimes home has a heartbeat."*

Tolkien, JRR. 1892-1973. (English writer, poet, philosopher.)
*"A single dream is more powerful than a thousand realities."*

Tolle, Eckart. "Born 1948. (A spiritual teacher and best-selling author. German-born resident of Canada.)
*"The light of consciousness is all that is necessary; you are the light."*

Tolstoy, Leo. 1828-1910. (Russian writer.)
*"Grow spiritually and help others to do so. It is the meaning of life."*.

Tzu. Lao. 500 B.C.E. (Ancient Chinese writer and philosopher.)
*"A journey of a thousand miles begins with a single step."*
*"Let it be still and it will gradually become clear."*

Walker, Alice. Born 1944. (American author.)
*"Peace will come wherever it is sincerely invited."*

Walsch, Neale Donald. Born 1943. (American author, screenwriter, actor, and speaker.)
*"Nothing in this universe occurs by accident."*

Woodson, Jacqueline. Born 1963. (American author.)
*"Even the silence has a story to tell you. Listen, listen, listen."*

Zinn, Jon Kabat. Born 1944. (An American professor emeritus of medicine.)
*"Breathe and let be."*

# CONTRIBUTING AUTHORS

**Best, Nancy**

*Nancy lives in central Colorado where she enjoys Zumba classes, playing pickleball, and reading books by Dr. Oliver Sacks. One day she hopes to be rescued by a cat.*

**Binder, Gail**

*Gail is a loving mother, grandmother, and great-grandmother. Her first 25 years of marriage were spent packing and repacking every two-three years and moving her family where the Air Force assigned her husband from one coast to the other and overseas twice. The next 25 years of marriage were spent packing and repacking to enjoy traveling on her terms with rivercruises, and adventures in faraway lands.*

**Bott, Dave**

*Dave is an avid cyclist, family man, public school educator, community volunteer, and has had first responder training. He enjoys discussions on spiritual experiences. Dave was the first "hero" on site in the rescue of Mike Gallagher as covered in "Two Men on a Mountain," in Chapter One.*

**Cason, Debby**

*Debby Cason loves Nature in all forms, even humans! For seven and a half years, Debby and her husband Roger sailed halfway around the world in a 40-foot sailboat. Roger is now wheelchair bound, and living in a nursing home, so Debby recommends living life to the fullest while you can. If you wish to read about their sailing adventures in Fiji, you can find* ***Swimming with Glory*** *available on Amazon.*

**Dorfmeister, Margery**

*Margery is a present-day Nonagenarian! Savvy with a delightful sense of humor, her creativity as a poet, playwright, author, freelance writer, and essayist has delighted audiences for years. She taught creative writing for Colorado Mountain College and was a radio news reporter. As a composer and lyricist who created many wonderful melodramas, she was co-creator and director of a local community theater group. She also enjoys painting beautiful watercolor scenes and knitting homespun prayer shawls.*

**Ellwood, Grover**

*Grover is 70 (years, that is), who occasionally attempts poetry, lives with his wife of almost 50 years, and tries to reflect on his blessings every day. He paints and plays guitar when Spirit moves him.*

**Gallagher, Mike**

*Mike is a free spirit who calls Colorado home. His amazing story of "Rescue, Recovery, and Faith," is detailed in his book,* ***Small Town, Big Rescue****. He still likes the "exhilaration of riding a good motorcycle on some good roads."*

**Fedora, Rosie**

*Rosie is a humanitarian and humorist who often draws on her experience as a long time Registered Nurse. Passionate about the power of creativity to heal and spread hope, Rosie often works collaboratively with other artists. A former New Yorker, Rosie enjoys exploring the west and southwest regions of the United States where she now lives.*

**Inada, Sally Small**

*Sally is a hard-core reader, writer, and needleworker. Her hobbies include napping, haiku, and dark chocolate. Her teen son says, "loving and caring mom for 16 years should be enough."*

**Jones, Nathan**

*Nathan is a father, husband, and wildlife biologist who enjoys exploring the Colorado mountains on two wheels or two skis.*

**Karlsson, T.T.**
*T.T. Karlsson is a retired teacher, author, and live music sponsor in a small town in the middle of Colorado. His book,* ***Bluebirds on the Roof****, is a compelling account of loss and grief, offering words of encouragement in hopes to offer comfort to others in their hour of greatest need.*

**Keidel, Jeff**
*Jeff still likes to catch snakes, bugs, and other wild critters; he caught Kathleene in 1982.*

**Keidel, Tyler**
*Tyler enjoys engaging in authentic conversations and helping others navigate life challenges.*

**Liebowitz, Jenny**
*Jenny is retired from a career in accounting and still enjoys her lifelong passion for tennis. She has added pickleball to her activities and is looking forward to more traveling adventures with her husband, Steve.*

**Liebowitz, Steven**
*For over 40 years Steven dedicated himself to public safety before retiring. He and Jenny, his wife of 43 years, enjoy their kids, grandkids, traveling, and playing pickleball.*

**Ohmstede, Jan**
*Jan retired from a career in education and traded technical writing for creative writing and poetry. After 21 years in Alaska, she resides in the mountains of Colorado and misses gigantic moose and the Aurora Borealis.*

**Reis, Laura**
*Laura is a creative spirit and dabbles in many art forms but is especially fond of leather art, jewelry making and mixed media. She lives in the Lost Sierra wilderness of California with her husband.*

**Ruiz, Barb**
*Barb lives in the Pacific Northwest with her husband and two cats. She enjoys gardening, hiking, biking, kayaking, and just about anything that involves sunshine.*

**Smith, Audrey**

*Audrey is a devoted wife, mother, and grandmother who values her relationship with her Savior in highest regard. She is a talented writer who draws on her life experiences from her years of living in South America and her love of family and friends.*

**Sorden, Christine**

*Christy loves talking to people about their spiritual experiences, believes in filling the world with kindness and goodness and that the universe often works in mysterious ways.*

**Walker, Amber**

*Amber is a physical therapist from Alaska who has a holistic wellness practice in Denver. She enjoys teaching medical courses and instructing SUP lessons and is the author of two books about chronic conditions:* ***Mast Cells United*** *and* ***The Trifecta Passport****. Amber's happy places are on a surfboard, paddleboard, or mountain trail!*

**Wallin, Caryl**

*Caryl resides in Tucson, Arizona, where she enjoys playing tennis and birding the sky islands. She resides with her three dogs: "Top Dog," husband Bill, yellow lab, Reacher, and Golden Retriever, Lacey.*

**Walters, Nancy**

*Nancy is a retired technical writer, interface designer, and instructor. She lived in Colorado until she retired to California where she still hikes in mountains but also walks for miles along Ventura Beach.*

**Weber, Maria**

*Maria moved from the Great Smoky Mountains to the Rocky Mountains in 1966. She lives with her husband and two cats where she enjoys writing fiction and poetry with a paranormal twist. Her memoir,* ***I'll Be There to Write the Story: A Mother-Daughter Journey Beyond Death****, was published in 2010 and won 2nd Place in Memoir and 3rd Place in Spirituality from the Colorado Independent Publishers' Association.*

# BIBLIOGRAPHY

Canan, Janine., Editor. *Messages from Amma*. Celestial Arts. Berkeley, California. 2004.

Dillard, Sherrie. *Discover Your Psychic Type*. Llewellyn Publications. Woodbury, Minnesota. 2019.

Feather, Dr. Sally Rhine. *The Gift*. St. Martin's Press. New York, New York. 2005.

Gawain, Shakti. *Living in the Light*. New World Library. San Francisco, California. 1998.

Gallagher, Mike. *Small Town, Big Rescue*. 27 Rivers Press. New York-London. 2018.

Karlson, T.T. *Bluebirds on a Roof*. Outskirts Press, Inc. 2018.

Maddox, Sylvia. "Where Can I Touch the Edge of Heaven?" www.explorefaith.org. 2004.

Moon, Kimberly. *Psychic Empath*. Coppell, Texas. 2020.

Shetty, Jay. *Think Like a Monk*. New York, New York. 2020.

Silva, Mari. *Astral Projection*. Made in USA, Columbia, SC. 2020.

Weber, Maria. *I'll Be There to Write the Story*. Pinon Valley Press. Buena Vista, Colorado. 2010.

**Websites:**

https://www.anthonychene.com Chen, Anthony Productions.

https://youtu.be/7nMeoT6TgNo IANDSvideos Life Reviews Peter Anthony and Tricia Barker.

https://youtu.be/W2QEXUIYL-U IANDSvideos Dr. Mary Neal.

https://youtu.be/tmT13Uuumpo IANDSvideos Anita Moorjani.

https://www.anthonychene.com The Nature of Consciousness - Interview with Alan Hugenot.

http://www.swedenborg.com/modern-spir... offTheLeftEye, YouTube. "Swedenborg and Life." Streamed September 15, 2015. Host Curtis Childs.

https://offtheleftey e.com/ A Guide to Spiritual Awakening - Swedenborg & Life. August 17, 2020.

https://youtu.be/hsZPTVpNBNs Only Human. January 9, 2018.

https://youtu.be/chA3A7Wcshc Akiane Kramarik. April 12, 2020.

https://youtu.be/zPB2ECoZ9z4 His Holiness Radhanath Swami. TEDx Talks. February 8, 2016.

https://youtu.be/PEmaWdfUUuk Searching For Light with Radhanath Swami | Rich Roll Podcast. September 3, 2020.

# ACKNOWLEDGEMENTS

Thank you to my beautiful daughter, Jennah Jones, and to my dear friends, Margery Dorfmeister and Jean Buster for your love and support by reading my manuscript and offering your suggestions. Gratitude also goes to my husband, Jeff, and son, Tyler, who offer their constant support and faith in me. My mother, Gail, sisters, Caryl, Jenny, and Laura, and my brothers, Chips and Christopher, thank you for extending your love and encouragement in so many ways. You are my touchstones! My friends who are my cheering squads behind the scenes include my weekly writing group, The Bloc: Marge, Maria, Stephanie, Judy, Jan, and Pat, thank you for adding writing inspiration and support every Monday morning. You light up the week! Thank you to all the authors who contributed to this project and trusted me with your work. I value each voice. And great gratitude goes out to all those who helped bring this book to print, especially Chrissy Cutting of Fiverr, and Ryan Scheife and Joanna Price of Mayfly Design.

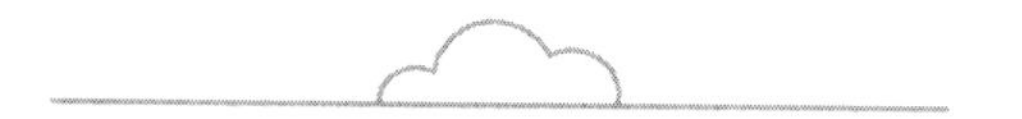

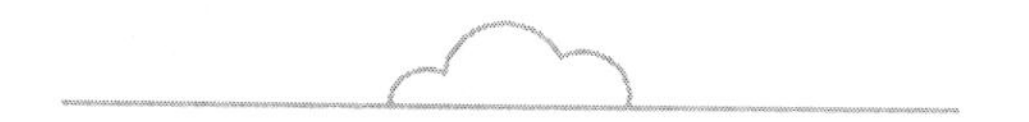